CAMPAIGN 367

THE FINNISH-SOVIET WINTER WAR 1939–40

Stalin's Hollow Victory

DAVID MURPHY

ILLUSTRATED BY JOHNNY SHUMATE
Series editor Nikolai Bogdanovic

OSPREY PUBLISHING
Bloomsbury Publishing Plc

Kemp House, Chawley Park, Cumnor Hill, Oxford OX2 9PH, UK
29 Earlsfort Terrace, Dublin 2, Ireland
1385 Broadway, 5th Floor, New York, NY 10018, USA
Email: info@ospreypublishing.com
www.ospreypublishing.com

OSPREY is a trademark of Osprey Publishing Ltd

First published in Great Britain in 2021

A catalogue record for this book is available from the British Library.

Print ISBN: 978 1 4728 4396 8
ePUB: 978 1 4728 4397 5
ePDF: 978 1 4728 4394 4
XML: 978 1 4728 4395 1

Maps by www.bounford.com
3D BEVs by Paul Kime
Index by Zoe Ross
Typeset by PDQ Digital Media Solutions, Bungay, UK
Printed and bound in India by Replika Press Private Ltd.

22 23 24 25 26   10 9 8 7 6 5 4 3 2

Artist's note

Readers can discover more about the work of illustrator Johnny Shumate at
the below website:
https://johnnyshumate.com

Osprey Publishing supports the Woodland Trust, the UK's leading woodland
conservation charity.

To find out more about our authors and books visit
www.ospreypublishing.com. Here you will find extracts, author
interviews, details of forthcoming events and the option to sign up for
our newsletter.

Author's acknowledgements

I would like to thank everyone at Osprey for their help and encouragement
in developing this project. In particular, my thanks go to Marcus Cowper
and Nikolai Bogdanovic for their help and patience. I was very glad that
Johnny Shumate was available to develop the colour plates and this has
resulted in excellent artwork. I also wish to acknowledge the help of Lenita
Taylor at the Finnish Embassy in Dublin and Colonel Pasi Saarikosi, the
defence attaché to the UK and Ireland. The assistance of Raija Ylönen-
Peltonen at the Finnish National Archives in Helsinki was much
appreciated. I would also like to thank Major Victor Milyutin, the former
assistant defence attaché at the Russian Embassy in Dublin. As always, I am
indebted to friends and family, especially my three special ladies –
Georgina, Ellie and Lottie. I dedicate this book to them.

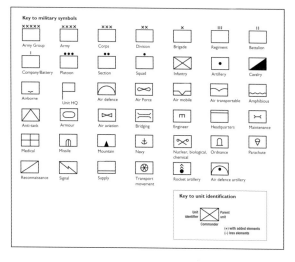

PREVIOUS PAGE
A Finnish soldier armed with a Suomi SMG. (SA-kuva)

CONTENTS

Finland, the USSR and Scandinavia in 1939

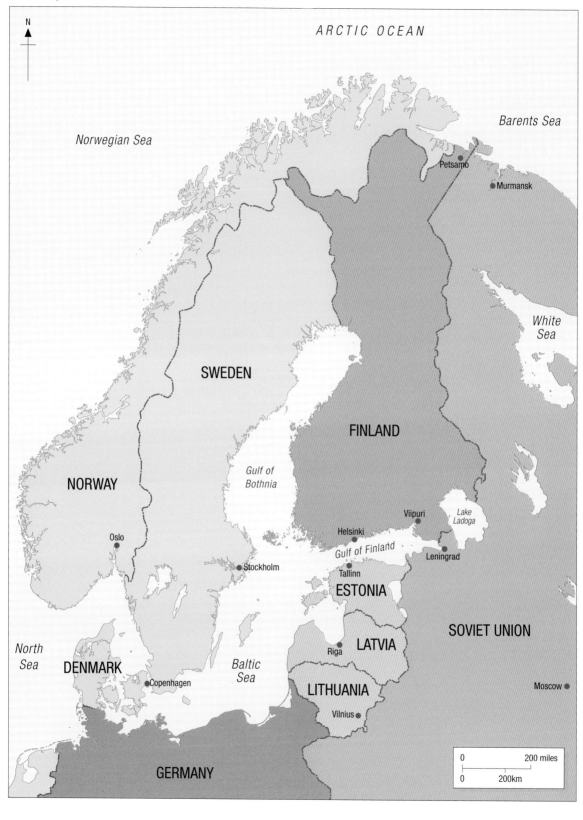

ORIGINS OF THE CAMPAIGN

Just over 80 years on, the Finnish-Soviet Winter War (November 1939–March 1940) remains a fascinating subject for historians, military practitioners and the general reader alike. Beginning just months after the start of World War II, the narrative of the larger conflict has often pushed the story of Finland's struggle against the numerically superior Soviet Red Army into the background. At the time, the war was the focus of political and public attention across Europe and the United States. Coming just months after the overrunning of Poland, the world waited to see if the tiny Nordic country could stand up to the Soviet juggernaut. The odds did not look good. In troop numbers alone, the Finns would field a maximum strength of around 300,000 during the war. The Soviets deployed around 450,000 in their initial attacks and their total strength during the course of the campaign rose to over 760,000. In terms of materiel, the statistics were equally startling. The combined Soviet field armies would employ over 6,500 tanks during the campaign. The Finns had only 32 obsolescent tanks when the war started, although they would later supplement their tank force with large numbers of captured Soviet tanks.

In November 1939, therefore, even the most optimistic observer would not have reckoned much on Finland's chances. Yet in the 105 days of conflict that followed, the Finnish Army managed not only to hold out but also to inflict large casualties on the Soviet. It was a classic 'David vs Goliath' military struggle and while the Soviets would eventually emerge victorious, it was at great cost in troops and equipment. The damage to the Red Army's credibility during the Winter War was equally significant and would inform Germany's later plans to attack the Soviet Union.

The Winter War arose out of a backdrop of long-term tensions. The territory that comprised Finland had been part of Sweden until 1809 when it was invaded by Russia. The key strategic reason for this was Russia's concerns about Finnish territory being used to mount an invasion into Russia in the direction of St Petersburg (a very similar rationale would be advanced in 1939). Russia then created the Grand Duchy of Finland, which would serve as a buffer state. In political terms, the Grand Duchy of Finland enjoyed considerable autonomy until the turn of the 20th century, at which point Russia began to exert its considerable influence in pursuit of its policies of 'Russification' within the territories of its empire. Within Finland, there were increasing calls for autonomy and independence, and the collapse of Tsarist Russia following the Bolshevik Revolution of 1917 facilitated this shift. In December 1917, the Finnish senate declared independence and the

Bolshevik government, realizing that it could not hold onto the new emerging state, recognized Finland's independence just a few weeks later. However, an internal civil war broke out between 'White' and Bolshevik elements and while this saw the defeat of the Bolshevik faction and the expulsion of its forces from Finnish soil, it was a bitter affair that resulted in internal tensions until the 1930s. It is estimated that around 40,000 people were killed or wounded in the Finnish Civil War.

Having gained full sovereignty in May 1918, Finland joined the League of Nations in 1920 and thereafter aligned closely with Sweden in mutual defence planning. However, in the immediate post-war years, tensions continued between Finland and Russia (post-1922, the Soviet Union). There were incursions of Finnish 'volunteers' into Russian territory in Karelia in 1918 and 1919 while, in 1920, a Russian plot to assassinate Field Marshal Carl Gustaf Mannerheim, the commander-in-chief of the Finnish White Guard, was uncovered. In October 1920, Finland and Soviet Russia signed the Treaty of Tartu and the historic border between the Grand Duchy of Finland and Tsarist Russia was accepted as being the new border between the two countries. Another favourable aspect of the treaty for Finland was the acquisition of the ice-free port of Petsamo on the Arctic coast. Yet tensions remained, with further border incursions by both sides in 1921 and 1922. In 1932, the two countries signed a non-aggression pact, and this was renewed in 1934.

Throughout the 1930s, Finland also faced internal tensions, and while the Finnish Communist Party had been banned in 1931, there were still clashes between socialist and right-wing groups. In 1932, there was a failed coup by the right-wing Lapua Movement, but as the Finnish economy improved, the domestic political landscape stabilized to some degree. On the eve of the Winter War, Finns were enjoying the first prolonged phase of economic prosperity since the end of World War I. In defence terms, there was a continued tension between factions in government and society, some of which believed that an avowed policy of neutrality was in itself a defence. Despite the turbulent international strategic situation throughout the 1930s, there was a reluctance on the part of the Finnish government to upgrade the army and to invest further in defensive fortifications. This was particularly true during the premiership of Aimo Cajander (1937–39), who refused to acknowledge Stalin's hostile intentions or to invest in the Finnish armed forces. Within the latter, Mannerheim as commander-in-chief constantly pressured a succession of governments for increased attention to the nation's defence. This was especially true during Cajander's coalition government. As the Finnish-Soviet relationship worsened, there was a late phase of hectic activity in September and October of 1939, and the number of bunker systems on the Karelian Isthmus increased from 168 to 221.[1]

Stalin's consolidation of power following the Great Purge of 1936–38 resulted in a shift of Soviet strategic priorities in the region. Ever-paranoid, Stalin was concerned about pro-Finnish elements on the Soviet side of the border and also that a Finnish-German alliance would result in an offensive from the Karelian Isthmus towards Leningrad, which lay only 32km inside Soviet territory. From April 1938, an initial contact was made by an NKVD agent, Boris Yartsev, with the Finnish foreign minister Rudolf Holsti. A mutual defence arrangement was suggested due to Soviet distrust of the Germans, but this would have entailed the leasing or ceding of Finnish territory in order to protect the approaches to Leningrad. Finland refused, and in the following months came under increasing pressure to cede territory in order to provide the Soviet Union with its desired buffer zone. Throughout 1938 and 1939, Soviet troop numbers continued to grow along the Finnish-Soviet border. As they were aware of the extent of the purges in the Soviet Union and also severe rural collectivization reforms, the Finnish government was decidedly unreceptive to Soviet assurances and demands. At the same time, Finland tried to redefine its defence arrangements with Sweden.

By 1939, Stalin had decided that the former Baltic territories of the Imperial Russian Empire needed to be repossessed in order to provide buffer states against German aggression. On 23 August 1939, the Molotov–Ribbentrop Pact was signed between Hitler's Germany and Stalin's Soviet Union. Technically a non-aggression pact, this treaty was designed to allow the two powers to cooperate in the reorganization of the Baltics and Eastern Europe in their favour. The German and Soviet delegations secretly divided these territories into spheres of influence and it was decided that Finland would fall within the Soviet sphere. The invasion of Poland on 1 September 1939, just a week after the signing of the Molotov–Ribbentrop Pact, not only led to the beginning of World War II but also caused a range of small states to revise their strategic plans. The speed of the German campaign in Poland, followed by the Soviet invasion of the eastern half of the country, indicated how future conflicts would be fought. For the Finns, the outcome was alarming, as the Polish Army was a much larger force than theirs in

---

1   It is interesting to note that Helsinki was the planned venue for the 1940 Summer Olympics.

Soviet motorcycle reconnaissance troops on parade in Red Square before the war. The Red Army had expanded its motor recce elements during the 1930s. However, in the terrain and conditions of the Winter War, such formations were largely useless. (Photo by Ivan Shagin/ Slava Katamidze Collection/ Getty Images)

terms of both manpower and equipment. If Poland was overrun so quickly, what chance would the Finnish Army have against a German or Soviet attack? Against this wider strategic backdrop, in September and October 1939, Estonia, Latvia and Lithuania signed mutual assistance pacts with the Soviet Union. Finland remained essentially unaligned and, startled by the outcome in Poland, it began a gradual mobilization under the pretence of organizing 'extraordinary' manoeuvres and additional training.

On 5 October 1939, the Soviets invited a Finnish delegation to Moscow to continue discussions on their territorial demands. The Finnish delegation, headed by the distinguished statesman Juho Kusti Paasikivi, met with Soviet officials on 11 October 1939 and was presented with a list of territorial demands. Paasikivi had held senior offices within the Finnish government since independence. He was a leading voice in the anti-Bolshevik faction during the civil war and was a tough and uncompromising negotiator. In turn, Stalin and Molotov were at times friendly and cajoling in their dealings with the Finns. At others, they were icily demanding. Among various demands, the Soviets wanted the border on the Karelian Isthmus to be pushed around 30km northwards and demanded that all fortifications on the isthmus be demolished. The Soviets also wanted the Finns to cede islands in the Gulf of Finland and the Rybachi Pensinula while also requesting to be allowed to lease the island of Hanko to establish a naval base. In return, the Soviets offered to cede territory in Eastern Karelia to Finland – in reality, this was more territory than the Finns were being asked to give away. However, the Soviet plan would have left Finland totally compromised at a strategic level, as the majority of their border defences fell within the zones to be ceded. The Soviet ultimatum caused considerable debate and division within the Finnish parliament, and negotiations continued until 13 November. As the Finnish delegation frantically tried to buy some extra time, its army continued preparing for the war that now seemed inevitable. In the latter phases of the talks, Reichsmarshall Hermann Göring was contacted by the Finns for his input in the hope that, considering the German-Soviet pact, he could de-escalate the situation. In a desperate last-minute measure, the Finns offered to cede the Terijoki district, which would have doubled the distance from

Finnish troops marching through Helsinki at the outbreak of the war. Their clothing and equipment would suggest that these are reservists who have been activated for the war. (Photo by Carl Mydans/The LIFE Picture Collection via Getty Images)

the Finnish border to Leningrad. This was rejected, and talks broke down on 13 November.

For almost two weeks after the end of the talks, Finland held its breath. Mannerheim, gauging correctly that the Soviets might try to contrive a border incident, ordered that all heavy guns be withdrawn out of range of the Finnish-Soviet border. Nevertheless, there was a shelling incident on 26 November at the border town of Mainila, in which, it was claimed, Soviet soldiers had been killed. Later research suggests that the Soviets had shelled their own territory, and archival sources cast doubt on the claim that any Soviet soldiers were killed at all. With predictable speed, the Soviets blamed the Finnish Army for a cross-border shelling at Mainila and, on 28 November, the Soviet government cut diplomatic links and cancelled the non-aggression pact with Finland. On 30 November, the Winter War began.

It is impossible in the course of this short book to cover the hundreds of actions of the Winter War. Therefore, this volume will focus on the main phases of operation, but in the hope that they also reflect the character of the wider war. Also, it should be noted that there are some points of contention among historians regarding some timings, unit sizes and also the responsibility for certain actions. Considering questions of access and veracity with respect to archival sources, it is likely that some issues will remain unresolved. A key example of this is the question of which side was responsible for the Mainila shelling incident that began the war. While the weight of evidence seems to suggest that the Mainila shelling was contrived by the Soviet Union as a *casus belli*, this remains a topic of debate even within the Russian historical community. What is certain is that, for the Finnish and Soviet soldiers on the ground, the Winter War was a harsh and bloody campaign that saw incredible acts of bravery and sacrifice on both sides. Many of these episodes have been lost to history, but it is worth keeping the experience of the common soldier in mind.

The Winter War produced a huge number of propaganda posters. Both the Finns and the Soviets engaged in a propaganda war and developed a whole range of posters. At an international level, several subscription funds were set up to help aid the Finnish war effort. This poster was developed for the London-based 'Finland Fund'. (Public domain)

CHRONOLOGY

1809   17 September: Treaty of Fredrikshamn. Following Russia's defeat of Sweden in the Finnish War of 1808–09, the autonomous Grand Principality of Finland is created within the Russian Empire.

1899   15 February: Declaration of the 'February Manifesto' by Tsar Nicholas II. The powers of the Finnish parliament or 'Diet' are curtailed. Russian Imperial law can now be imposed within Finland.

1908–17   Period of 'Russification' – Finnish autonomous powers are gradually removed and all political and state matters come under Russian control.

1914–18   Martial law declared throughout Finland during World War I. Russification programmes are cancelled for the duration of the war.

1915   The Jäger movement is established and the first groups of volunteers travel to Germany for training.

1917   The February Revolution in Russia begins a gradual reduction of Russian control over Finland.

18 July: The Finnish parliament declares itself to be the sole source of state power within Finland.

7 November: The 'October Revolution' in Russia.

6 December: Finnish Declaration of Independence.

31 December: Bolshevik government in Russia recognizes Finnish independence.

1918   25 January: The Finnish Civil Guard is established.

27 January–14 May: Finnish Civil War between White (Civil) Guard and Red Guard; over 38,000 casualties in total. These casualties include over 500 Red prisoners who are executed and over 12,000 who die of hunger and disease in POW camps.

21 March–2 October: Attempt to annex territory on the Karelian Isthmus from Russia. Further expedition to Petsamo.

9 December: Prince Frederick Charles of Hesse is appointed as king of Finland.

14 December: Frederick Charles abdicates following collapse of the German Empire. Carl Gustaf Mannerheim is appointed as regent.

1918–22   The 'Kinship Wars' (*Heimosodat*): Finnish volunteers conduct incursions into Karelia, Ingria and Estonia.

1919   Finland declares itself to be a republic.

1920   14 October: Treaty of Tartu ends state of conflict between Finland and Russia. Petsamo is ceded to Finland while Russia retains the territories of Repola, Porajärvi and North Ingria. East Karelia remains an area of contention.

1921–22   Rebellion in Karelia against Soviet authority. Units of Finnish volunteers assist but without official state backing.

1929–32	Rise of the nationalist and right-wing Lapua Movement.
1932	21 January: Finland signs a non-aggression pact with the Soviet Union.
	27 January–6 March: failed right-wing rebellion by the Lapua Movement. The movement is disbanded.
1934	7 April: Finland and the Soviet Union extend their non-aggression pact to 1945.
1935	August: Commissar Andrew Zhdanov carries out a survey of Finnish-Soviet border as an initial planning phase for invasion.

1939

17 April	Britain and France open discussions with the Soviet Union.
23 August	Germany and the Soviet Union sign the Molotov–Ribbentrop non-aggression pact. In secret clauses, Finland, the Baltic States, Poland and Romania are divided into Soviet and German spheres of interest.
1 September	Germany invades Poland, beginning World War II.
17 September	Soviet forces begin occupying Eastern Poland.
19 September	Finland declares neutrality.
28 September	Soviet-Estonian non-aggression pact.
5 October	Soviet Union announces that it wishes to discuss territorial concessions by Finland.
9 October	Finnish delegation under Juho Kusti Paasikivi travels to Moscow.
10 October	Finnish Army begins 'extraordinary reservist manoeuvres'.
13 November	Finnish-Soviet discussions in Moscow end without resolution.
26 November	Soviets blame the Finnish Army for a cross-border shelling incident at Mainila.
28 November	The Soviet government ends all diplomatic negotiations and renounces the non-aggression pact.
30 November	The armies of the Soviet Leningrad Military District begin an invasion of Finland along the entire length of the Finnish-Soviet border. The Finnish capital Helsinki is bombed.
1 December	The Soviets announce the formation of a pro-Soviet puppet Finnish government. In Finland, Prime Minister Risto Ryti's cabinet is announced.
3–6 December	Finnish delaying forces fall back on the defences of the 'Main Line'.
4–6 December	Soviet troops advance on the Main Line of the Mannerheim defences.
6 December	Soviet forces begin the first of a series of failed attacks on the Mannerheim Line. Both France and Britain declare that they will send military aid to Finland.

14 December	The Soviet Union is expelled from the League of Nations.
22 December	A Finnish counter-attack advances to the Aittojoki River and digs in.
23 December	A failed Finnish counter offensive, nicknamed by the Finns as the 'idiot's nudge', achieves little gain.
27–29 December	The successful Finnish attack at Suomussalmi begins a Soviet reversal. The Soviet 163rd Rifle Division suffers heavy losses in the fighting around the town.
30 December	Finnish attacks begin on the 44th Rifle Division, which is strung out along the Raate Road.

1940

3–4 January	Attempts to airdrop supplies to the isolated elements of the 44th Rifle Division along the Raate Road. Some units are successfully resupplied.
6 January	Finns cut the Raate Road at several points. The 44th Rifle Division is divided into a number of *motti* (total encirclements).
7 January	*Motti* of the 44th Rifle Division are reduced. Finns capture the majority of the division's equipment and transport vehicles. Army Commander, 1st Class Semyon K. Timoshenko is appointed to command the Soviet north-west group of forces.
8 January	End of the Battle of Suomussalmi. The final elements of the 167th and 44th Soviet Rifle divisions are mopped up. The Finnish government offers to open peace negotiations.
9 January	Elements of the Soviet 168th Rifle Division are isolated in *motti* on the Pitkäranta Road.
29 January	The Soviet government agrees to begin peace negotiations.
1 February	The Soviet 7th and 13th armies, under Timoshenko, begin an offensive on the Karelian Isthmus, crossing the frozen ice at Viipuri Bay.
4 February	Trapped Soviet troops in the Lemetti *motti* surrender.
5 February	France and Britain confirm plans to send a force to aid the Finns.
8–11 February	Strong Soviet attacks in the Taipale and Summa sectors. Both offensives see heavy Soviet use of artillery.
11 February	The Soviet 123rd Rifle Division breaches the Mannerheim Line near Summa. Fall of the Poppius Bunker. Finnish attacks on encircled *motti* of Soviet troops at Suanajärvi.
12 February	Via Swedish intermediaries, the Soviet government offers peace terms to Finland. Heavy air and artillery attacks support the Soviet drive on Viipuri.
13 February	Soviet 13th Army achieves a major breakthrough on the Mannerheim Line at Lähde. Despite Finnish counter-attacks, Soviet forces develop this breakthrough into a breach several kilometres wide.
15 February	Finnish units withdraw to the Interim Line of defences. Soviet troops trapped in a *motti* at Uomaa break out and return to their own lines.

17 February	Finnish withdrawal to the Interim Line is completed. Soviet units trying to break out of the Rykmentti *motti* are effectively destroyed. The Soviet offensive in the Taipale sector intensifies.
22 February	Soviet attacks on the Interim Line intensify. General Axel Heinrichs replaces General Hugo Österman as commander of Finnish forces on the Karelian Isthmus.
23 February	Remaining Soviet troops in the Rykmentti *motti* withdraw, leaving their severely wounded behind.
26 February	Battle of Honkaniemi. This is the only time that Finnish forces (II Corps) use a tank force in the Winter War. The Finnish armour is defeated, losing five out of six tanks.
27 February	Under increasing Soviet pressure, units of the Finnish I and II corps start to abandon the Interim Line and begin a phased withdrawal to the rear defensive line – the Rear Line.
28 February	Soviet forces pass the Interim Line and refocus their offensive on Viipuri. A Swedish volunteer force is sent to the Salla sector to aid the defence.
29 February	Soviet forces occupy the entire length of the Interim Line and begin operations on the Rear Line around Äyräpää. Over 3,000 surrounded Soviet troops try to break out from the Lemetti *motti* in two groups; one of these is destroyed. With hopes of significant foreign intervention fading, the Finnish government decides to enter into peace talks with the Soviet Union.
1–6 March	Increasing Soviet pressure in the Viipuri sector. On 6 March, a Finnish peace delegation leaves for Moscow.
7 March	The British general Sir Edmund Ironside informs the Finnish government that Britain intends to send military aid and also troops. Heavy Soviet offensives in the Kollaa sector and also on the islands in Viipuri Bay.
9 March	Soviet units sever the Hamina–Viipuri Road. Fighting for Viipuri intensifies as Mannerheim refuses to order a withdrawal from the city. The last Finnish reserves are committed.
10 March	Finnish counter-attacks in the Kollaa River sector are repulsed. Finnish withdrawal to final defensive positions.
11 March	Desperate fighting takes place around Viipuri.
12 March	General Heinrichs orders a withdrawal from Viipuri. The Finnish and Soviet negotiators sign the Moscow Peace Treaty.
13 March	A ceasefire comes into effect at 1100hrs (Finnish time). Despite the ceasefire, Soviet troops continue to attack Viipuri until the city is captured.
15 March	Finnish troops withdraw to the new border lines established under the Moscow Peace Treaty.
	Beginning of the 'Interim Peace'. This will last until 29 June 1941.

1941

29 June	Beginning of the Continuation War.

OPPOSING COMMANDERS

SOVIET

For the Soviet Union, supreme command of the army rested with **Joseph Stalin** and he was the prime mover in the campaign against Finland. For strategic reasons already outlined, he desired to control Finland and also the Baltic States to serve as buffer zones against any attack from the West. While usually cast as a paranoid aggressor in histories of this war, in Stalin's defence he was aware of the links between Finland and Germany that had developed in the 1930s. These included technical collaboration on submarine projects. There was also a personal backstory for Stalin: in 1917, he had been sent to Finland to acknowledge the Finnish declaration of independence but also with instructions to try to keep them within the Russian sphere of influence. It was a mission in which he had failed.

During both the Russian Civil War and the Russo-Polish War, Stalin had held military command and therefore had some actual military experience. Stalin's behaviour in both of these campaigns was typified by a hard-line attitude towards subordinate commanders and also troops under his

Joseph Stalin pictured with the German foreign minister Joachim von Ribbentrop (with arms folded) in 1939. Following Soviet success in Poland, Stalin turned his gaze towards the Baltic States and also Finland. He was the prime mover in the plan to invade Finland, with the strategic intention of developing a buffer state to the west of the USSR. (Corbis via Getty Images)

command. He showed himself not to be adverse to ordering assaults that resulted in high casualties, nor to the execution of deserters and defectors. Stalin also engaged in purges of his officer corps during this early phase of his career. All of these trends would re-emerge once Stalin rose to power following Lenin's death in 1924.

From a military perspective, the Great Purge (1936–38) was particularly damaging, as Stalin ordered the liquidation or imprisonment of many in the top tier of the Soviet high command, including leading theorists such as Mikhail Tukhachevsky and Aleksander Svechin. Throughout the 1920s and 1930s, Soviet commanders had been developing theories of operational art and 'deep battle' in order to harness the potential of massed air power and armoured formations. When discussing future war, Soviet commanders planned for large-scale, sequential operations that would overwhelm key targets and destroy any enemy's capacity to resist. The essence of deep battle focused

on audacity, speed and initiative at all levels. These concepts were enshrined in the PU-36 – Provisional Field Regulations of the Red Army 1936. While the lessons of the Spanish Civil War (1936–39) were still being debated, the purges were beginning. Alongside the human suffering involved, from the Red Army's perspective the purges represented a criminal waste of many of its most talented commanders. The Great Purge was particularly ill-timed as it came during a period when the Red Army was undergoing a massive expansion from 1.3 million soldiers in 1937 to a planned 4.5 million in 1941. So, while the Red Army looked most impressive in terms of numbers, it was actually in a highly disorganized state during a key period of expansion and doctrinal reform.

On the eve of the Winter War, therefore, Stalin was enjoying a level of false confidence. The recent victory over the Japanese at Khalkhin Gol (May–September 1939) and the success in Poland led him to believe that an invasion of Finland would present little difficulty. In reality, the Soviet command was riven by factions, and once the campaign began, the senior commanders showed an inability to be imaginative and flexible in battle.

During the course of the Winter War, the Red Army would ultimately field two teams of army commanders. The first team became a byword for poor planning and leadership, and in January 1940, Stalin would bring in a second team in an effort to turn the campaign around for the Red Army. In 1939, the commander-in-chief of the Soviet Army was **Marshal Kliment Voroshilov** and he was the titular leader of the first cohort of generals. Voroshilov had been involved with the Bolshevik movement since 1904 and had held two army commands during the Russian Civil War. Trusted by Stalin, he was seen as being politically and militarily sound, but it is apparent now that he did not apply himself with enough rigour to the planning for the Finnish operation.

Marshal Kliment Voroshilov, commander of Soviet forces in the initial phases of the Winter War. A veteran of the Russian Revolution and the Russian Civil War, Voroshilov was close to Stalin and therefore avoided the purges of the late 1930s; indeed, he actively denounced colleagues during the process. His organization of training within the expanding Red Army was poor, and it is now generally accepted that his planning and handling of the Winter War was shambolic. He would eventually be removed from command and scapegoated for the poor Soviet performance. (Three Lions/Hulton Archive/ Getty Images)

Army Commander, 1st Class Semyon Timoshenko (right). Following the reversals of the early months of the campaign, Timoshenko was placed in command of the Red Army in 1940. He planned a rapid phase of reorganization and training, and this, combined with more effective tactical methods, would lead to Soviet success in March 1940. (Bettmann via Getty Images)

The responsibility for the operation was assigned to the Leningrad Military District under **Army Commander, 2nd Class Kirill Meretskov**. Like many of his associates, Meretskov had a good political pedigree and had been involved with the Bolshevik movement since 1917. He had served during the Russian Civil War and had passed through the Military Academy (later the Frunze) in 1921. During the Spanish Civil War, he had served as an advisor to the Republican government, using the pseudonym 'General Pavlovich'. On paper, therefore, Meretskov seemed to have the leadership and organizational capacity for this operation. In reality, he seems to have been detached from the planning process while also overestimating the potential of the raw, untrained troops under his command.

Under Meretskov's command, there were four further army commanders. These were **Army Commander, 2nd Class Vsevolod F. Yakovlev** (7th Army), **Division Commander Ivan N. Khabarov** (8th Army), **Corps Commander Mikhail P. Dukhanov** (9th Army) and **Corps Commander Valerian A. Frolov** (14th Army). These four commanders all had military experience dating back to the Russian Civil War period and were politically acceptable to Stalin. In Dukhanov's case, his military experience started in 1918 when he joined the Tsarist Army. It is certain that Yakovlev faced the toughest assignment, as 7th Army was tasked with breaking through the Mannerheim Line. All of these commanders were best suited to developing a methodological attack, making best use of their overwhelming numbers and their advantage in materiel. Ultimately, the Finnish Army and the terrain of the battlefield denied them the opportunity to develop such attacks.

Within the Red Army there was also a cohort of commanders who favoured the fluid and rapid deployment of air and armour assets across the width and depth of an enemy defence. Since the early 1930s, the Red Army had been developing the doctrine of 'deep battle'. The key advocate in this principle had been Mikhail Tukhachevsky, who had been 'purged' in 1937. Ironically, it was an adherent of this style of mobile warfare, **Army Commander, 1st Class Semyon Timoshenko**, who was appointed to take over the stalled offensive in 1940. Timoshenko's service dated back to World War I, where he had served in the Tsarist Army before joining the Bolsheviks, and he had seen considerable service in the Russian Civil War. Timoshenko, as a loyal supporter and friend of Stalin, was appointed to take over command of Soviet forces in January 1940. During his tenure the Red Army would be rapidly reformed and retrained in order to maximize its advantage in the renewed campaign.

Soviet leadership in the Winter War was initially unimpressive. Yet it is certain that many junior leaders displayed good leadership, although this fact is often lost in the long catalogue of operational errors and poor command. Once led competently, the Red Army showed itself to have considerable combat potential.

FINNISH

The commander-in-chief of the Finnish forces, **Field Marshal Carl Gustaf Emil Mannerheim** (1867–1951), had also begun his military career in the Tsarist Army, and in the intervening years had gained vast experience while also showing formidable qualities of command. Of German descent, his family were prominent in Sweden and also associated with the Grand Duchy of Finland from its foundation in 1817. Mannerheim's early years were somewhat turbulent and he managed to get expelled from the Hamina Cadet School in 1886. Following training at a private military lyceum, he was admitted to the Nicholas Cavalry School in St Petersburg and was commissioned into the Chevalier Guard Regiment in 1891. Present at the coronation of Tsar Nicholas II in 1896, Mannerheim enjoyed close links with the royal family. Following service in the Russo-Japanese War (1904–05), he undertook an espionage mission travelling from St Petersburg to Peking, via Tibet. On the outbreak of World War I, he was a major-general in the royal entourage and in command of the Guards Cavalry Brigade. He served on the Austro-Hungarian and Romanian fronts, but following the February Revolution in 1917, fell out with the Kerensky government and retired as a lieutenant-general. Returning to Finland, he became fully involved in the chaotic politics of that period, emerging as the military leader within the reactionary 'White' faction. By early 1918, Finland had descended into a

Field Marshal Carl Gustaf Mannerheim, commander-in-chief of the Finnish forces. A commander of considerable experience dating back to Tsarist service during World War I, Mannerheim displayed great strategic skill during the Winter War. His aristocratic lineage provided considerable scope for Soviet propagandists, but he earned the respect of his troops and also erstwhile opponents within Finland. (Bettmann via Getty Images)

bloody civil war between the White and Red factions, the latter being supported by Russian forces, while the Whites were supported by Swedish volunteers and by German funding and training. In March 1918, German troops landed at Helsinki, yet Mannerheim did not support the Finnish government's pro-German line. At the end of the civil war in June, he left for Sweden before travelling to London in October 1918 to gain recognition from Britain, France and the USA for the emerging new nation. In December 1918, he was elected as regent but lost in the first Finnish presidential election of July 1919, being beaten by Kaarlo Juho Ståhlberg, a prominent liberal nationalist.

Due to the bitter and bloody nature of the Finnish Civil War, Mannerheim was frequently targeted by internal socialist propaganda, and also the Russian propaganda machine, as an oppressor of the working classes. His aristocratic lineage and bearing did not help him in this regard. During the 1920s, he shunned politics and ignored overtures from right-wing elements. However, in 1931 he was appointed to Finland's Defence Council, and he was made field marshal in 1933. In the run-up to the Winter War, he had frequent clashes in cabinet as he pushed for further defence expenditure and reform. In October 1939, Mannerheim had

Lieutenant-General Hugo Österman, commander of Finnish troops on the Karelian Isthmus. An able commander, at various occasions during the campaign Österman clashed with Mannerheim, and he would eventually leave his command following the breach of the Karelian defences in 1940. (Corbis via Getty Images)

actually resigned, but accepted the role of commander-in-chief in November following the Soviet attack. In the months that followed, he would emerge as a unifying force and ultimately as a national hero. Throughout the war, he showed a realistic grasp of strategy and a willingness to cede territory that was not key and could not be defended. The desperate position of the Finns generated a series of crises that Mannerheim handled with an air of steely calm. He has since been criticized for not deploying reserves quickly and for leaving some Finnish units to fight unsupported. The operational reality was that Mannerheim had no major reserve formations to deploy by 1940.

Among Mannerheim's senior commanders, there were also some common factors regarding their previous service. The majority of corps, division and regimental commanders had served during World War I with the Finnish Jäger movement. At the beginning of World War I, Germany had indicated its support for an independent Finland and somewhere between 1,000 to 2,000 young Finns travelled clandestinely to Germany to undertake 'scout' or 'pathfinder' training. This was a front for military training as light infantry, and many of these Finnish volunteers went to serve in the 27th Prussian Jäger Battalion. They saw service on the Eastern Front before returning to Finland in early 1918 to take part in the Finnish Civil War. Their involvement in the civil war was decisive, and well-trained, the members of the Jäger movement rose within the army leadership.

Lieutenant-General Hugo Österman (1892–1975) had perhaps the most difficult assignment within the Finnish Army. A veteran of the Jäger movement, he had remained in the army after the civil war and was appointed commander-in-chief in 1933. With the rank of lieutenant-general, he took command of the Army of the Isthmus at the beginning of the Winter War. It was here that the main fortifications of the Mannerheim Line had been built, as it was expected to be the focus for the main Soviet effort towards Viipuri. Under his command, Österman had six divisions split into two corps commanded by lieutenant-generals Harald Öhquist and Erik Heinrichs, both of whom were also veterans of the Jägers and the Civil War. Österman was an organized and competent commander but clashed frequently with Mannerheim, whose early plans factored in an offensive action. These, Österman thought, were highly unrealistic for outnumbered formations who had no experience of engaging tanks. He also differed with Mannerheim on the role of reserve troops and defensive deployments. His role as commander-in-chief was made difficult due to Mannerheim's authority on the Defence Council. Having offered his resignation as early as December 1939, Österman finally stood down in 1940. He later held a series of administrative positions, including acting as Mannerheim's personal envoy to Wehrmacht HQ in 1944, before retiring in 1946.

Österman was succeeded as commander on the Karelian Isthmus by **Lieutenant-General Erik Heinrichs** (1890–1965). Heinrichs was unusual within the Finnish general staff as he had completed an advanced staff course in France in 1921. At the outbreak of the war, he was inspector-general of infantry and was appointed to command III Corps on the isthmus. He succeeded Österman as commander on the isthmus on 19 February 1940 and later went on to have a distinguished career during the Continuation War (1941–44).

The Finnish IV Corps, deployed on a 100km front north of Lake Ladoga, was commanded by **Major-General Woldemar Hägglund** (1893–1963), who had attended the Swedish Military Academy from 1931 to 1932. He was a determined commander and would distinguish himself at the Battle of Kollaa, in reality a series of engagements that ran throughout much of the Winter War. The final senior commander of the initial Finnish line-up was **Major-General Wiljo Tuompo** (1893–1957), who commanded the North Finland Group. This formation of activated reservists, border guards and civic guards held a front of over 950km north of Hägglund's IV Corps. Also a former Jäger, Tuompo had held command of the Border Guards from 1935. He and his men would use the forbidding terrain of northern Finland to great effect against the Soviet invaders.

There were obviously many other more junior commanders in the Finnish Army at the time – far too many significant leaders to all be mentioned here. Many officers of quite junior rank would display outstanding leadership at crucial times in the war. Among the more inspirational commanders, one must mention **Major-General Paavo Talvela**, who had seen service with the Jägers and in the Civil War before resigning from the army in 1919. He became involved in the Kinship Wars of the 1920s, which sought to incorporate other groups of Baltic Finns within a Greater Finland concept. These activities included incursions into Soviet territory. Re-joining the army, Talvela completed an artillery course in Wales (1923) before undertaking a general staff officers' course at the Finnish Academy (1926). Having resigned yet again, he was appointed as commander of Group Talvela, a mixed, corps-sized formation, at the start of the war. His victory at the Battle of Tolvajärvi was a huge morale boost for the entire country.

Finally, it should be pointed out that, while the Finnish Army was generally under-resourced in the 1920s and 1930s, officers at the General Staff Academy spent considerable time considering future wartime scenarios. As early as 1926, Paavo Talvela and Aaro Pajari presented theses on possible offensive operations in the Ladoga Karelia sector. They were then both relatively junior officers, but they would serve in the rank of major-general (Talvela) and lieutenant-colonel (Pajari) in the Winter War. In later peacetime exercises and wargames, scenarios were developed for defending Karelia and also central and northern Finland. Following a tradition of 'educating and training to fight', the Finnish staff were not, therefore, operating in an intellectual vacuum once hostilities began in 1939.

Major-General Johan Woldemar Hägglund (left), commander of the Finnish IV Corps, and Lieutenant-Colonel August Kuistio (right), in March 1940. Hägglund was a veteran of the 27th Prussian Jäger Battalion during World War I and had seen service in the Finnish Civil War. He played a prominent role in the defence of Kollaa. (SA-kuva)

OPPOSING FORCES

SOVIET

As was traditional in Russia from Tsarist times, the Red Army was a conscript force based on the mass induction of young men from designated military districts. Young men were eligible for two years conscripted service from age 19 and were drawn from the peasantry and urban working classes. There was a tendency to send conscripts from the rural labouring class to the infantry branch, while factory workers were sent to mechanized and technical units. The recruitment and training of officers remained a major problem for the Red Army throughout the 1930s, despite the fact that there was an extensive system of military academies across the Soviet Union. The lower aristocracy and bourgeois classes who had formed the officer class pre-Revolution were not deemed politically suitable, while the poor conditions within the army were well known and not an encouragement towards a military career. Even before the purges, there were over 10,000 unfilled junior officer posts, and the lack of leadership was exacerbated by the process of expansion. Officer courses were shortened to two years maximum, while some promising NCOs were also sent for officer training. However, the whole NCO concept was not well developed within the Red Army, as it was seen as a politically undesirable tier between soldier and officer. A cohort of strong NCOs – usually a vital component of modern armies – was sadly lacking. The end result of the purges and the problems with officer recruitment was a lack of leadership at both the senior and junior levels. A further complication came in the form of the political commissars appointed to every unit from company level upwards. They would act as a significant hindrance once the campaign began.

Training within the Red Army during this period was quite haphazard. The training of new conscripts took place within the units to which they were assigned, and this was left

to individual commanders to organize. There was no army-wide system of training or even any comprehensive system within the Leningrad Military District. Levels of training in basic small-unit tactics varied wildly across the army, and considering the short notice allowed to raise and recruit units for the Finnish offensive, some troops had just a couple of weeks training before the war began. Some Soviet POWs would later state that they had been rounded up on the streets of Leningrad, put into uniform and sent to the front just days

Soviet army musical instruments, captured following an action early in the war. The Finns were amazed that Soviet troops lacked the basic equipment required for survival, yet carried useless items such as these. (SA-kuva)

before the war began. The training required to coordinate large attacks combining air elements, artillery, tank and mechanized formations was almost unheard of.

In terms of personal weapons, the majority of Soviet riflemen were equipped with the 7.62mm Mosin-Nagant rifle. These tended to comprise the M1891/30, although some mechanized troops were issued with the carbine version, the M1938. Some units were equipped with the 6.5mm Fedorov Avtomat, a semi-automatic rifle that had been developed during World War I and was originally intended to be deployed as a crew-served weapon. The Fedorovs had been stockpiled and were generally issued due to the shortage of submachine guns (SMGs); only limited numbers of the PPD-34 and PPD-38 SMG types were available. The 7.62mm SVT-38 semi-automatic rifle also saw its combat debut in the Winter War. It proved to be a cumbersome, unreliable weapon and was unpopular with the troops, many of whom reverted to the bolt-action M1891/30 if possible as it was a much more reliable weapon in the winter conditions. Some of the M1891/30 and SVT-38 rifles were fitted with sniper scopes. The drum-fed 7.62mm DP-27 (Degtyaryov) machine gun was the most numerous infantry support weapon, while the PM M1910, the Soviet version of the Maxim heavy machine gun, was still in service and was used in large numbers. As support weapons, the Red Army had access to a range of mortars in calibres of between 50mm and 120mm. The 50mm RM-38, based on the British Stokes mortar, was the most portable and useful in the campaign. Grenades, when available, were generally of the RGD-33 fragmentation type.

The Soviets would field a large force, and communications were a vital element. Overall, there was a shortage of communications staff and a lack of artillery and forward air observers. A rifle regiment was assigned a signals company while a division had a signals battalion. These establishments would prove insufficient. Within armoured formations, radios were only fitted in command vehicles. Encoded communication systems proved to be unsecure, with the Finns often being able to decode signals. Some communications were still sent 'in clear'. Throughout the campaign, the Soviets continued to show a reliance on runners and flare and flag signals.

Given the timing of the offensive, it is now generally accepted that the Red Army was totally unprepared for a winter campaign. There was a lack of protective winter clothing – padded jackets, felt boots, etc. There was also a lack of snow suits for concealment on operations. Training in the use of skis was an afterthought, with a new training pamphlet *Ski-Training in the RKKA* coming to print in late October. At its most basic level, there was no training or equipping to allow Soviet soldiers to survive, manoeuvre and fight in the imminent winter conditions. Medical arrangements and logistics in general were overstretched from the beginning of the campaign and would eventually break down entirely. All objective assessments of the Soviet units ear-marked for this operation would suggest that morale was low at all levels of the organization.

On the plus side, the Red Army had quantity, a quality always approved of by Stalin. The initial force would number over 425,000 soldiers supported by over 2,500 tanks and thousands of aircraft. The numbers of artillery pieces, anti-tank artillery, heavy MGs and mortars similarly ran into the thousands. Soviet aircraft, such as the Tupolev SB bomber and the Polikarpov I-16 fighter, were among the most modern then available. Soviet tanks such as the T-26 and BT-7 were considered among the most advanced in the world. The Soviet high command was also confident that Soviet naval elements were vastly superior to the tiny Finnish Navy. So, while the Red Army may not have been in a position to engage in the highly mobile operations outlined in its own deep battle doctrine, it was felt that a slow, methodological advance of a mass army, shielded by tanks and artillery support, would prove successful.

FINNISH

The Finnish Army of the 1930s was also based on a conscription model, following lines largely set down within European armies during the 19th

The Lahti-Saloranta M/26 in action. Although an excellent support weapon, it was not available in enough numbers, and Finnish troops supplemented it with captured Soviet weapons. (SA-kuva)

century. All young men were liable for military service from the age of 18 for a period of 350 days. Those chosen for NCO or officer training were enlisted for 440 days. In subsequent years, all trained men were liable to periodical call-ups for major exercises or refresher training. All reserve units were established on a localized basis, allowing troops to be familiar with the terrain in which they would operate, and also allowing for greater unit cohesion. Initial training was undertaken in centralized recruit depots during soldiers' original phase of enlistment. This allowed for greater understanding of small-unit tactics, and reserve units could then practise such operations in their home area of operations.

A Finnish soldier armed with a Suomi SMG. The Finns used these excellent SMGs to deadly effect. (SA-kuva)

Specialized training camps were established for such weapons as the Bofors 37mm anti-tank gun, mortars or the Suomi KP/-31 submachine guns, and these programmes included reservist training. This allowed for the dissemination of knowledge throughout the army with respect to both weapons and tactics. One significant disadvantage lay in the area of anti-tank warfare. Due to the low number of tanks within the Finnish Army, few soldiers had exercised with or even seen a tank. This would prove to be an influential factor in the early days of the war.

The common soldier within the Finnish system differed from his Soviet counterpart in a number of ways. The majority of Finnish soldiers were from rural backgrounds and were inured to

Soviet troops examine a captured Finnish armoured train, 1940. Equipped with field guns and machine guns, such trains could pose considerable difficulties for attacking troops. This is a still from the Soviet newsreel film entitled 'The Mannerheim Line'. (Sovfoto/Universal Images Group via Getty Images)

One of the many junior leaders who distinguished himself in the war, Captain Aarne Juutilainen, the 'Terror of Morocco'. A veteran of the French Foreign Legion, he displayed impressive leadership and gallantry during the campaign. (SA-kuva)

the harsh Finnish winters. Many were accomplished hunters, and all Finns, including city dwellers, enjoyed a tradition of outdoor pursuits (camping, skiing and hiking) and in all weathers. They were, quite simply, equipped to survive in winter conditions and were capable of remaining operational. Their natural temperament made them ideal for hit-and-run operations in the wooded terrain, and they made ideal snipers. Throughout the war, the Finnish soldiers showed excellent initiative and were innovators in tactical terms, especially in the realm of tank killing and booby-trapping.

As mentioned previously, there was a strong cadre of leadership formed around veterans of the Jäger movement and also those who had served in the Civil War. In the 1930s, officer and NCO schools had turned out a strong cohort of junior leaders. By 1939, over 7,000 officers and 170,000 NCOs had passed through their respective training schools. Moreover, in both the officer and NCO programmes, the candidates were trained on a 'two-up' system – preparing them to step into more senior command positions if required.

In terms of personal equipment, the 1930s had seen a lack of defence expenditure, a fact frequently raised by Mannerheim. As a result, about 35 per cent of the troops activated in 1939 were issued with just a rifle, ammunition belt and a hat – or a Finnish cockade to apply to their own civilian hat. This was derisively referred to as the 'model Cajander', after Prime Minister Aimo Cajander who oversaw a particularly miserly phase of defence spending.[2] Many troops, therefore, would see out the war using their own civilian clothing and hiking equipment – haversack, boots, skis, etc. Thankfully, due to the Finnish affinity with the outdoors, this expedient seemed to work. The army could also supply white snow suits and smocks, which gave the Finns an initial advantage in the winter fighting.

Due to Finland's former history within the Russian Empire, there were large stocks of the M1891 Mosin-Nagant rifle available, and the Finns would also make use of thousands of Soviet weapons captured in the campaign. During the 1920s and 1930s, the Finns had also produced their own version of the Mosin-Nagant, and this was a far superior weapon in terms of both finish and performance. It was not available in enough numbers to equip all troops, but the M28/30, originally designed for the Civic Guard, was the most numerous. The standard SMG was the 9mm Suomi KP/-31, and this weapon achieved a formidable reputation during the war, being eventually copied by the Soviets in their PPD-40 and PPsh-41 models. Although available in only limited numbers at the start of the war, the KP/-31 proved to be particularly effective in the close fighting conditions, and provided much-needed firepower to Finnish squads. Light and portable, it was highly favoured by mobile ski units. The 7.62mm Lahti-Saloranta LS/26 machine gun was the standard infantry support weapon, although this, too, was not available in enough numbers, with Finnish troops making use of captured Soviet automatic weapons, in particular the DP-27. Versions of the Maxim gun were also used throughout the army and there were two Finnish versions in 7.62mm: the models M-09/21 and M-32/33. There were also small numbers of a German version in 8mm. Versions of these were fitted on skis and sleds during the forest fighting. The standard-issue grenade was the M-32 stick grenade, although the Finnish soldiers would make extensive use of Molotov cocktails and other improvised devices.

Finally, no Finnish soldier would take the field without a version of the traditional knife – the *puukko*. The bayonet seems to have been totally shunned in favour of these knives. These

A Finnish gun crew with a 76 K/02. There were around 180 of these 76mm guns in Finnish service, many dating to 1918. (SA-kuva)

A group of volunteers from the women's Lotta Svärd organization; in this case, acting as aircraft spotters for the Finnish air defence. They would also serve in medical and other auxiliary military units. (Keystone-France/Gamma-Keystone via Getty Images)

2   The supply of a national cockade met the most basic requirements of the Hague Conventions regarding the identification of combatants.

were personal items and many different variations can be observed in photos of the period. They would be used to some effect in close-quarter fighting. John Langdon-Davies, the British writer and war reporter, later wrote of the use of these knives by Finnish soldiers (Langdon-Davies 1941, pp. 23–24). In his travels across the battlefront, he met members of Finnish patrols who claimed to have dispatched entire Soviet MG crews, and captured the gun, using nothing more than their *puukkos*. In psychological terms, the reputation of the use of *puukkos* played greatly on Soviet fears of knife-wielding Finnish patrols roaming in the darkness.

It is also true to say that, overall, there was a sense of national identity among the Finnish soldiers that was missing on the Soviet side, facilitated by the uniquely Finnish characteristic – *sisu* (guts). Morale was good in the army, and it was supported by a Civil Guard component and a women's movement – the Lotta Svärd. These two formations played a significant role in the war.

The Civil Guard was a separate organization to the army and dated back to the Civil War period, where it had emerged from White Guard and other independent military groups. From these paramilitary beginnings, a more formal force evolved after the war that was part youth-training organization and part local defence force. The Civil Guard ran training programmes and shooting and skiing competitions – all designed to increase the military competence of its members – and these were open to the army. Some Civil Guard members held army rank, and this allowed for mutual training schemes. The organization had its own logistical and weapons repair facilities and even redesigned the Mosin-Nagant rifle to produce the excellent M28/30 'Civil Guard rifle'. Trained in basic infantry tactics and military fortification,

Finnish dog handlers with their messenger dogs. (SA-kuva)

Civil Guard members played a major role in the upgrading of the Mannerheim Line in 1939. Constantly training and with immediate access to their own weapons, they could be mobilized quickly. There were about 120,000 members at the start of the war, and the youngest and fittest of these, about 65,000, served alongside the army. Formed in 1921, the Lotta Svärd had over 60,000 women in the organization during the 1930s. During the Winter War, members of the Lotta Svärd served as nurses, in auxiliary military services and in munitions production.

Further contingents of Border Guards or Frontier companies also augmented the army. In 1939, five Guerrilla (Sissi) battalions were formed from second-line and over-age

A Finnish sniper holding a captured Soviet sniper rifle, Suomussalmi, December 1939. Scoped rifles were not common in the Finnish Army, and captured weapons were often used. (SA-kuva)

contingents. Intended to work as insurgent, 'stay-behind' troops, they would actually be used as a reserve cadre.

However, in numerical terms, there were serious shortfalls. In the entire war, the Finns could only muster around 340,000 troops. Artillery and artillery shells were in short supply, with much of the artillery stock dating to before World War I. For example, the most common field gun was the 76mm K/02, an inheritance from the pre-1914 Tsarist regime. There were 192 of these guns, representing about one-third of the available artillery. Anti-tank artillery was in especially short supply with only 50 Bofors guns (37mm) being available alongside small numbers of 20mm L39 Lahti anti-tank rifles. Numbers of tanks were small and, depending on sources, there were between 26 and 32 tanks available. These were mostly of the obsolete Renault FT-17 type alongside six British Vickers Mark Es (6-ton). Neither tank was a match for the Soviet designs. The Finnish Air Force had a mere 114 aircraft, although these would put in an impressive performance. Field telephone and radio equipment were in short supply, but as the campaign developed, the Finns made use of captured Soviet equipment and also the civilian telephone network. The Finnish Army medical facilities were generally good but became more challenged as the war progressed, despite the effort of female volunteers from the Lotta Svärd movement. Logistics were mainly horse-drawn but the Finns also had the capacity to move supplies by sleds of different sizes largely regardless of the weather. These could be towed by men on skis, ponies or even reindeer. The Finns also had the capacity to develop heated tents or dug-outs in the field, which increased the survivability of their troops and troop morale.

ORDER OF BATTLE, 30 NOVEMBER 1939

SOVIET RED ARMY
Leningrad Military District (Army Commander, 2nd Class Kirill Meretskov)

7TH ARMY (KARELIAN ISTHMUS)

Commanding officer: Army Commander, 2nd Class Vsevolod F. Yakovlev
19th Rifle Corps (Division Commander Filipp N. Starikov)[3]
24th Rifle Division
    7th Rifle Regiment
    168th Rifle Regiment
    274th Rifle Regiment
    160th Artillery Regiment
    246th Howitzer Regiment
    315th Tank Battallion
43rd Rifle Division
    65th Rifle Regiment
    147th Rifle Regiment
    181st Rifle Regiment
    162nd Artillery Regiment
    200th Howitzer Regiment
    369th Tank Battallion
70th Rifle Division
    68th Rifle Regiment
    252nd Rifle Regiment
    329th Rifle Regiment
    221st Artillery Regiment
    227th Howitzer Regiment
    368th Tank Battallion
123rd Rifle Division
    245th Rifle Regiment
    255th Rifle Regiment
    272nd Rifle Regiment
    323rd Artillery Regiment
40th Tank Regiment
    155th Tank Battalion
    157th Tank Battalion
    160th Tank Battalion
    161st Tank Battalion
50th Rifle Corps (Division Commander Filipp D. Gorolenko)
49th Rifle Division
    15th Rifle Regiment
    212th Rifle Regiment
    222nd Rifle Regiment
    31st Artillery Regiment
    166th Howitzer Regiment
    391st Tank Battalion
90th Rifle Division
    173rd Rifle Regiment
    286th Rifle Regiment
    588th Rifle Regiment
    96th Artillery Regiment
    149th Howitzer Regiment
    339th Tank Battalion
142nd Rifle Division
    19th Rifle Regiment
    461st Rifle Regiment
    701st Rifle Regiment
    334th Artillery Regiment
    260th Howitzer Regiment
    445th Tank Battalion
35th Tank Regiment
    105th Tank Battalion
    108th Tank Battalion
    112th Tank Battalion
10th Armoured Corps (Division Commander Prokofy L. Romanenko)
1st Tank Regiment
    4th Tank Battalion

8th Tank Battallion
19th Tank Battallion
13th Tank Regiment
    6th Tank Battallion
    9th Tank Battallion
    15th Tank Battallion
7th Army Reserve
138th Rifle Division
    554th Rifle Regiment
    650th Rifle Regiment
    768th Rifle Regiment
    295th Artillery Regiment
    436th Tank Battallion
20th Tank Regiment
    90th Tank Battallion
    91st Tank Battallion
    95th Tank Battallion
    301st Armoured Car Battalion

8TH ARMY (LADOGA KARELIA)

Commanding officer: Division Commander Ivan N. Khabarov
1st Corps (Brigade Commander Roman I. Panin)[4]
139th Rifle Division
    364th Rifle Regiment
    609th Rifle Regiment
    718th Rifle Regiment
    354th Artillery Regiment
155th Rifle Division
    436th Rifle Regiment
    659th Rifle Regiment
    786th Rifle Regiment
    306th Artillery Regiment
    421st Tank Battalion
56th Corps (Division Commander Aleksandr I. Tcherepanov)
18th Rifle Division
    97th Rifle Regiment
    208th Rifle Regiment
    316th Rifle Regiment
    3rd Artillery Regiment
    12th Howitzer Regiment
    381st Tank Battalion
    201st Flame-thrower Tank Battalion
56th Rifle Division
    37th Rifle Regiment
    184th Rifle Regiment
    213rd Rifle Regiment
    113th Artillery Regiment
    247th Howitzer Regiment
    410th Tank Battalion
168th Rifle Division
    367th Rifle Regiment
    402nd Rifle Regiment
    462nd Rifle Regiment
    453rd Artillery Regiment
    392nd Howitzer Regiment
    378th Tank Battalion
    456th Tank Battalion
8th Army Reserve
75th Rifle Division
    28th Rifle Regiment
    34th Rifle Regiment
    115th Rifle Regiment
    68th Artillery Regiment
    235th Howitzer Regiment
    21st Tank Battalion
    111th Tank Battalion
    274th Tank Battalion
    218th Flame-thrower Tank Battalion

---

3 Division Commander rank was equivalent to major-general.

4 Brigade Commander rank was equivalent to brigadier-general.

9TH ARMY (CENTRAL FINLAND)

Commanding officer: Corps Commander Mikhail P. Dukhanov[5]

47th Corps (Division Commander I. F. Dashitshev)

122nd Rifle Division
    420th Rifle Regiment
    596th Rifle Regiment
    715th Rifle Regiment
    273rd Mountain Rifle Regiment
    285th Light Artillery Regiment
    100th Tank Battalion

163rd Rifle Division
    81st Rifle Regiment
    662nd Rifle Regiment
    759th Rifle Regiment
    365th Artillery Regiment
    365th Tank Battalion

Special Corps (Division Commander M. S. Shmyrov)

54th Rifle Division
    118th Rifle Regiment
    337th Rifle Regiment
    529th Rifle Regiment
    86th Artillery Regiment
    97th Tank Battalion

44th Rifle Division (in transit)
    25th Rifle Regiment
    146th Rifle Regiment
    305th Rifle Regiment
    122nd Light Artillery Regiment
    179th Howitzer Regiment
    312th Tank Battalion

14TH ARMY (LAPLAND)

Commanding officer: Corps Commander Valerian A. Frolov

14th Rifle Division
    135th Rifle Regiment
    325th Rifle Regiment
    143rd Artillery Regiment
    241st Howitzer Regiment

52nd Rifle Division
    58th Rifle Regiment
    112th Rifle Regiment
    205th Rifle Regiment
    158th Artillery Regiment
    208th Howitzer Regiment
    349th Tank Battalion
    411th Tank Battalion

104th Mountain Rifle Division
    95th Rifle Regiment
    217th Mountain Rifle Regiment
    242nd Mountain Rifle Regiment
    290th Artillery Regiment

FINNISH ARMY

KARELIAN ISTHMUS

Commanding officer: Lieutenant-General Hugo Österman

I Corps (Lieutenant-General Harald Öhquist)

4th Division
    10th Infantry Regiment
    11th Infantry Regiment
    12th Infantry Regiment
    4th Field Artillery Regiment
    4th Light Detachment
    5th Bicycle Battalion

5th Division
    13th Infantry Regiment
    14th Infantry Regiment
    15th Infantry Regiment
    5th Field Artillery Regiment
    5th Light Detachment
    1st Heavy Artillery Battalion

    2nd Heavy Artillery Battalion
    3rd Heavy Artillery Battalion

11th Division
    31st Infantry Regiment
    32nd Infantry Regiment
    33rd Infantry Regiment
    11th Field Artillery Regiment
    11th Light Detachment

U-Group
    Uudenmaar Dragoon Regiment
    Häme Cavalry Regiment
    3rd Infantry Battalion
    7th Infantry Battalion
    1st Jäger Battalion

M-Group
    1st Infantry Battalion
    4th Infantry Battalion
    3rd Jäger Battalion

L-Group
    2nd Infantry Battalion
    5th Infantry Battalion
    2nd Jäger Battalion

III Corps (Lieutenant-General Erik Heinrichs)

8th Division
    23rd Infantry Regiment
    24th Infantry Regiment
    25th Infantry Regiment
    8th Field Artillery Regiment
    8th Light Detachment

10th Division
    28th Infantry Regiment
    29th Infantry Regiment
    30th Infantry Regiment
    10th Field Artillery Regiment
    10th Light Detachment
    4th Heavy Artillery Battalion

R-Group
    3rd Field Replacement Brigade
    6th Infantry Battalion
    4th Jäger Battalion
    3rd Brigade Artillery Battalion

Reserves
    1st Division
    1st Field Replacement Brigade
    2nd Field Replacement Brigade
    1st Brigade Artillery Battalion
    2nd Brigade Artillery Battalion
    3rd Brigade Artillery Battalion

LADOGA KARELIA

IV Corps (Major-General Juho Heiskanen; from December 1939, Major-General Woldemar Hägglund)

12th Division
13th Division

NORTH FINLAND GROUP

Commanding officer: Major-General Wiljo Tuompo
Lapland Group (based in Salla and Petsamo)
North Karelian Group

ARMY RESERVES

Commanding officer: Marshal Carl Gustaf Mannerheim
6th Division
9th Division
1 x Field Replacement Brigade

---

5   Corps Commander rank was equivalent to lieutenant-general.

OPPOSING PLANS

SOVIET

Soviet plans for an invasion of Finland arose from Stalin's desire to create a series of buffer zones along the western borders of Soviet territories. Therefore, in its essence, the strategic goal was powered by fundamentally the same principles that had led to the creation of the Grand Duchy of Finland during the 19th century. Also, following World War II, the creation of the Soviet Bloc created a large buffer zone between the USSR and its former Western allies. The strategic imperatives in these cases were very similar.

While the Soviets had been putting Finland under some pressure in the preceding years, the outbreak of World War II increased Stalin's determination to bring Finland under Soviet control. Also, in September and October 1939, Latvia, Lithuania and Estonia had been pressured into signing mutual defence agreements and had allowed the deployment of Soviet troops within the Baltic States. Finland remained an outlier, and Stalin feared a move through Finnish territory to attack the Soviet Union; his catalogue of potential enemies included both the Allies and Nazi Germany. The train of Stalin's strategic logic made the invasion of Finland inevitable, and it was his intention, once he had secured control of the country, to have it run by a puppet Finnish government.

Like their German counterparts, the Soviet high command, Stavka, was practised in developing strategic plans in peacetime. The initial planning for the Soviet invasion of Finland actually was begun in 1936 and some outline scenarios were developed. Evidence would suggest that the initial Soviet plan envisaged a highly controlled and gradual occupation of Finland, taking the nature of the terrain into account. This more cautious approach did not suit Stalin, however, and he demanded a more dramatic plan. Ultimately, responsibility for the invasion was handed over to the Leningrad Military District under the command of Army Commander, 2nd Class Kirill A. Meretskov.

Plans were hastily put together in November 1939, and it is now generally accepted that the Soviets grossly underestimated the Finnish terrain, fortifications and also the quality of their army. Chief Marshal of Artillery Nicholas N. Voronov later recalled a November 1939 planning meeting in his memoirs and was astounded at the casual way that potential difficulties were dismissed out of hand. Asked for his time estimate for the operation, he suggested two to three months, but was told by Commissar for Defence Gregory I. Kulik: 'Marshal Voronov – you are ordered to base all your

The Soviet attack plan

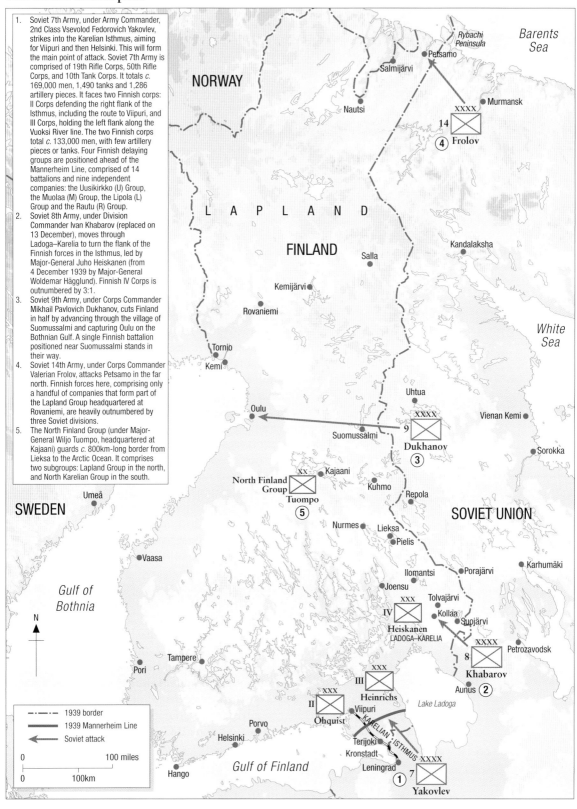

1. Soviet 7th Army, under Army Commander, 2nd Class Vsevolod Fedorovich Yakovlev, strikes into the Karelian Isthmus, aiming for Viipuri and then Helsinki. This will form the main point of attack. Soviet 7th Army is comprised of 19th Rifle Corps, 50th Rifle Corps, and 10th Tank Corps. It totals *c.* 169,000 men, 1,490 tanks and 1,286 artillery pieces. It faces two Finnish corps: II Corps defending the right flank of the Isthmus, including the route to Viipuri, and III Corps, holding the left flank along the Vuoksi River line. The two Finnish corps total *c.* 133,000 men, with few artillery pieces or tanks. Four Finnish delaying groups are positioned ahead of the Mannerheim Line, comprised of 14 battalions and nine independent companies: the Uusikirkko (U) Group, the Muolaa (M) Group, the Lipola (L) Group and the Rautu (R) Group.
2. Soviet 8th Army, under Division Commander Ivan Khabarov (replaced on 13 December), moves through Ladoga–Karelia to turn the flank of the Finnish forces in the Isthmus, led by Major-General Juho Heiskanen (from 4 December 1939 by Major-General Woldemar Hägglund). Finnish IV Corps is outnumbered by 3:1.
3. Soviet 9th Army, under Corps Commander Mikhail Pavlovich Dukhanov, cuts Finland in half by advancing through the village of Suomussalmi and capturing Oulu on the Bothnian Gulf. A single Finnish battalion positioned near Suomussalmi stands in their way.
4. Soviet 14th Army, under Corps Commander Valerian Frolov, attacks Petsamo in the far north. Finnish forces here, comprising only a handful of companies that form part of the Lapland Group headquartered at Rovaniemi, are heavily outnumbered by three Soviet divisions.
5. The North Finland Group (under Major-General Wiljo Tuompo, headquartered at Kajaani) guards *c.* 800km-long border from Lieksa to the Arctic Ocean. It comprises two subgroups: Lapland Group in the north, and North Karelian Group in the south.

Soviet troops and tanks during a bridging exercise in the summer of 1939. While the Red Army could carry out such operations with a high degree of effectiveness during manoeuvres, the frequent water obstacles of the Finnish terrain proved difficult. In this case, the tanks are the twin turret version of the T-26. (Sovfoto/Universal Images Group via Getty Images)

estimates on the assumption that the operation will last a maximum of 12 days' (Nenye et al 2015, p. 50). For his part, Meretskov had been told to secure Finnish capitulation by Stalin's 60th birthday on 21 December 1939. Showing catastrophic levels of hubris, plans were made for the seemingly inevitable victory parade in Helsinki and a special piece of music by Shostakovich was commissioned to be played at the ceremony. As it was later remarked, the Red Army invaded Finland equipped with brass bands and printing presses but without winter clothing, skis, white paint to camouflage their tanks and vehicles and other key equipment for a winter campaign.

On paper, the Soviet plan looked sound, and four armies, numbering over 400,000 troops, would take part in the initial invasion. The main effort would be on the Karelian Isthmus and this was allocated to the 7th Army under Army Commander, 2nd Class Vsevolod F. Yakovlev. This army was tasked with clearing the Mannerheim Line defences, taking Viipuri and then moving on Helsinki. The Soviet 8th Army, under Division Commander Ivan N. Khabarov, was to focus its attack to the north of Lake Ladoga and, having broken through, to drive into the interior. The exploitation of a breakthrough here also offered the possibility of sweeping southwards into the rear of the Finnish defenders on the Karelian Isthmus. The Soviet 9th Army, under Corps Commander Mikhail P. Dukhanov, was given the town of Oulu on the coast of the Gulf of Bothnia as its objective. If successful in seizing Oulu, the 9th Army would effectively cut Finland in two at its narrowest point. Finally, the Soviet 14th Army, under Army Corps Commander Valerian A. Frolov, was to cooperate with the Soviet Northern Fleet and focus on the Petsamo region. The successful capture of Petsamo would deny Finland any possibility of receiving foreign aid by sea, while it would also remove the possibility of a Finnish move on Murmansk. While intelligence on the Finnish Army and defences was far from comprehensive and the effect of terrain and weather had been grossly underestimated, the Soviet high command was confident that their plans offered every chance of success.

FINNISH

The Finnish commanders enjoyed a far lesser range of options and this was very apparent to their commander-in-chief, Field Marshal Mannerheim. On the Karelian Isthmus, the relatively constrained space meant that engaging in a guerrilla campaign was not practicable. Here the campaign would be more conventional, and the Finnish shortage of men and equipment, especially artillery, would push the defenders to their limits. The fortifications of the Mannerheim Line were set back from the actual Finnish-Soviet border. This would allow for an initial phase of resistance wherein the Finns traded space for time, before falling back on their fortified lines. Outside Karelia, the Finnish defence would rely on the ability of its formations to manoeuvre in the inhospitable terrain in order to stop Soviet columns and then reduce

Finnish defences on the Karelian Isthmus

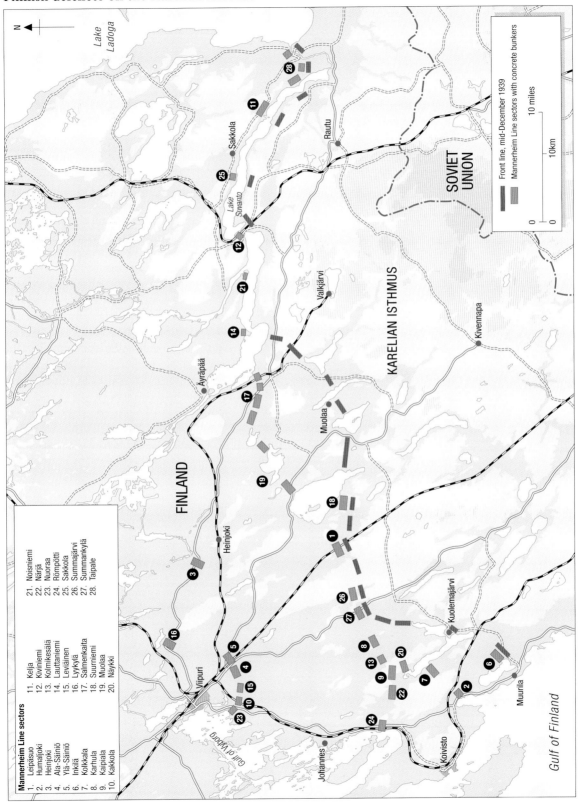

Mannerheim Line sectors

1. Leipäsuo
2. Humaljoki
3. Heinjoki
4. Ala-Säiniö
5. Ylä-Säiniö
6. Inkilä
7. Kolkkala
8. Karhula
9. Kaipiala
10. Kakkola
11. Kelja
12. Kiviniemi
13. Kolmikesälä
14. Lauttaniemi
15. Leväinen
16. Lykylä
17. Salmenkaita
18. Suurniemi
19. Muolaa
20. Näykki
21. Noisniemi
22. Närjä
23. Nuoraa
24. Römpötti
25. Sakkola
26. Summajärvi
27. Summankylä
28. Taipale

Front line, mid-December 1939

Mannerheim Line sectors with concrete bunkers

them. Finnish formations, sometimes operating similarly to guerrilla-type units, would need to stop the Soviets at choke points before breaking up their attacks. Pre-war planners had developed two operational plans on the Finnish side: *Venäjän Keskitys* (VK) 1 and 2 (VK stands for 'Soviet concentration').

VK1 planned for offensive action in the context that the Soviet Union was also involved in campaigns on other fronts. VK2 planned for a defensive posture and predicted heavy fighting on the Karelian Isthmus and also around Lake Ladoga. Due to the difficulty of the terrain, it was assumed in VK2 that the northern territories would not be the focus of a major attack.

In the wider strategic sense, Mannerheim knew that Finland had only three options: (1) Resist and delay in the hope of foreign intervention. (2) Resist as strongly as possible in order to prompt a peace overture from Stalin. (3) Fight to the bitter end.

Ultimately, the tone of the Winter War would equate more to the latter option. Hopes of foreign intervention on a scale that would tip the balance in Finland's favour gradually evaporated. Norway and Sweden maintained a neutral stance, and while the League of Nations would expel the Soviet Union due to its aggression, in reality it could only stand by impotently as events developed. Both France and Britain would later promise military aid, but both were at war with Germany and had little, if anything, to spare. However, the ad hoc nature of the Soviet planning effectively cancelled out their numerical and materiel advantages. The Finnish terrain also reduced the effectiveness of Soviet tanks, artillery and air power. So, the Finnish plan, which focused on maximizing terrain advantages to increase the effectiveness of their dogged, defensive stance, would come to dominate the initial phase of the conflict despite other disadvantages.

It has been argued that the Finns followed a Fabian strategy – trading space for time and avoiding contact to preserve their forces. The history of the Winter War contradicts this suggestion, as the Finns were ultimately extremely aggressive in their strategy, attacking and counter-attacking whenever the opportunity presented in order to wear down the Soviet attackers.

Finnish troops exercising in gas masks. Despite fears that the Red Army would use chemical weapons, this never came to pass in the Winter War. (Photo by Three Lions/Hulton Archive/ Getty Images)

THE WINTER WAR

OPENING MOVES

On the morning of 30 November 1939, the armies of the Soviet Leningrad Military District began an invasion of Finland along the entire length of the Finnish-Soviet border, which stretched for approximately 1,300km. The four assigned armies (7th, 8th, 9th and 14th) made their initial advances along eight main routes of access running from the Karelian Isthmus up to the north of Finland. These armies were composed of 21 divisions; in all, over 450,000 troops. There was no formal declaration of war.

In a sinister precursor to later air attacks throughout World War II, the Finnish capital city Helsinki was bombed twice during the first day. The initial attack occurred at 0900hrs and was timed to coincide with rush hour. The attack killed many civilians, while no military targets were hit. Facing international criticism, the Soviet foreign minister Vyacheslav Molotov later claimed that the Soviet Air Force was not bombing Finnish cities but rather dropping humanitarian aid. Thenceforth, the Finns would refer to Soviet aerial bombs as 'Molotov's bread baskets'. The war correspondent Martha Gellhorn wrote about the first day's bombing, noting that the second raid of the day, which came around 1500hrs, was not announced by an air raid siren. The Soviet planes had infiltrated undetected and dropped their bombs at the low level of 200m. The raid lasted just one minute but, as Gellhorn noted, 'It was the longest minute anyone in Helsinki had ever lived through' (Gellhorn 2016, p. 57).

In a typical political move, on 1 December the Soviets established a puppet government, the Finnish Democratic Republic, under Otto Kuusinen at Terijoki on the Karelian Isthmus. This small town had fallen to the Soviets on day one of the war and the puppet government was henceforth known as the 'Terijoki government'; however, it gained no public support within

A Finnish cavalry soldier. The Finns would make extensive use of horses for scouting, dispatch riding and also logistical units. (SA-kuva)

Finland, nor did it become a rallying point for internal dissent against the legitimate government. As Finland prepared for the coming struggle, a new cabinet formed under Risto Ryti while Field Marshal Mannerheim was confirmed as commander-in-chief. Throughout the duration of the war, Finland would continue in diplomatic discussions with friendly nations while also protesting its case to the League of Nations, from which the Soviet Union was expelled on 14 December.

For the Red Army, the Karelian Isthmus was chosen as the location for the initial main effort. If the Mannerheim Line could be passed, Soviet forces could push towards Viipuri, the capture of which would open a route to Helsinki. In strategic terms, this axis of advance offered the prospect of a swift and decisive campaign. This task was assigned to the Soviet 7th Army under Army Commander, 2nd Class Vsevolod F. Yakovlev and, in all, over 250,000 Soviet troops were allocated to this offensive. However, while well-supplied in terms of men, artillery, tanks, air support and other equipment, the 7th Army had only formed up in Leningrad on 14 September 1939, a bare six weeks before the invasion. As a formation, its troops were untrained and inexperienced when it came to carrying out a major, combined-arms operation. Following a heavy artillery barrage, the 7th Army crossed the border on the morning of 30 November.

Facing them were around 130,000 Finnish troops in defensive positions running from the Gulf of Finland to Lake Ladoga. These were formed into II Corps (Öhquist) and III Corps (Heinrichs). The Mannerheim Line defences were located back from the actual Finnish-Soviet border at distances of 30km to 75km depending on location. The Finns intended to use this space well and deployed around 21,000 troops as part of four delaying groups designated after their commanders as groups U, L, M and R. The intervening territory had been heavily laid with mines, booby-traps, tank obstacles and barbed-wire entanglements. There was also a high number of snipers deployed, and it was hoped that the delaying groups and the associated battlefield obstacles would blunt the initial Soviet attack.

Despite these measures, the Soviet troops made good progress, often aided by the heroic efforts of their combat pioneer crews in clearing the various obstacles. Having never encountered tanks before, several Finnish units broke and fled, while in some cases there were retirements due to confusion over orders. Mannerheim was furious as the battlefield space that had been so carefully prepared to create delay was given up so easily. By 5–6 December, the Soviet 7th Army had largely passed through the delaying zone and was preparing to assault the main defences of the Mannerheim Line. The speed of the advance led Meretskov, commander of the Leningrad Military District, to intervene in 7th Army deployments. He decided to create a dedicated assault force to bring overwhelming pressure on the eastern section of the line – the Taipale sector. This 'Right Wing' force combined the 49th Rifle Division, 150th Rifle Division and the 19th Rifle Regiment. In support were the 50th Rifle Corps, the 142nd Rifle Division and the 90th Rifle Division. Meretskov thought that such a concentration of force would crack the line in the Taipale sector while also serving to draw Finnish forces away from the left and the centre of their line. Such pressure might also facilitate the offensive of the 19th Rifle Corps in the direction of Viipuri. The Soviet 10th Armoured Corps was moved up in expectation of a breakthrough and exploitation phase. In preparation for their offensive, the Soviets put down a 40-hour artillery barrage.

Despite a vast inferiority in terms of numbers and all kinds of materiel, the Finns possessed some local advantages in the Taipale sector. There were a number of water features – the Vuoksi and Taipale rivers and also lakes Suvanto and Ladoga – and these had extensive trenchworks developed on their northern shores. Projecting towards the Taipale River was a promontory of marshland known as Koukkuniemi over which Soviet divisions would have to cross, having cleared the river. The terrain itself was hard-going for infantry and virtually impossible for armour, while the Finns had pre-ranged their artillery on the promontory and also possible routes across Lake Suvanto. The whole zone chosen by Meretskov for a decisive blow was therefore perfectly designed as a killing ground, despite Finnish misgivings about the strength of the local defences. Both of the local Finnish divisional commanders, colonels Claës Winell (8th Division) and Viljo Kauppila (10th Division), were veterans of 27th Prussian Jäger Battalion.

The Soviet attack, and its repulse, that developed between 6 and 27 December highlighted the various command and tactical difficulties that would dog the initial phases of their campaign. The crossing of the Taipale River on 6 December by regiments of the 49th Rifle Division (15th, 222nd and 212th) went

Medical officer and members of the Lotta movement beside a Finnish hospital train. (Bettmann via Getty Images)

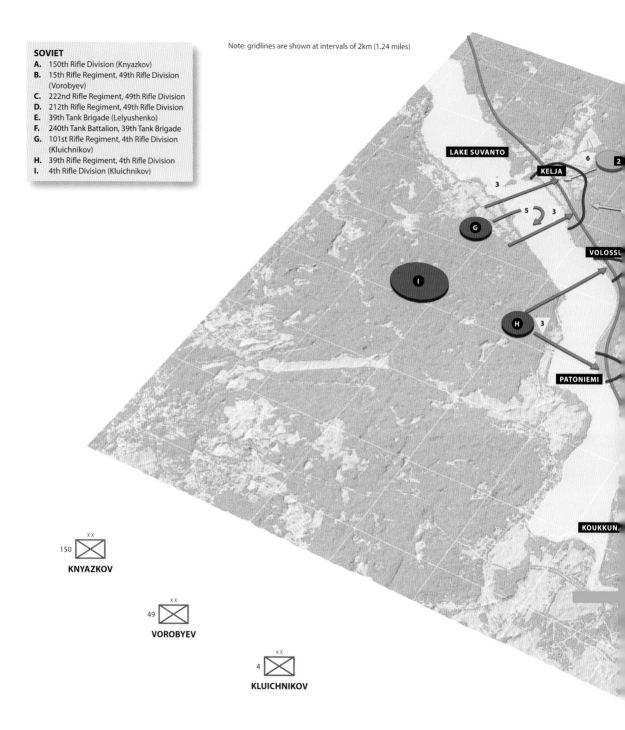

SOVIET
A. 150th Rifle Division (Knyazkov)
B. 15th Rifle Regiment, 49th Rifle Division (Vorobyev)
C. 222nd Rifle Regiment, 49th Rifle Division
D. 212th Rifle Regiment, 49th Rifle Division
E. 39th Tank Brigade (Lelyushenko)
F. 240th Tank Battalion, 39th Tank Brigade
G. 101st Rifle Regiment, 4th Rifle Division (Kluichnikov)
H. 39th Rifle Regiment, 4th Rifle Division
I. 4th Rifle Division (Kluichnikov)

LAKE SUVANTO

KELJA

VOLOSSU

PATONIEMI

KOUKKUN

150 XX
KNYAZKOV

49 XX
VOROBYEV

4 XX
KLUICHNIKOV

▼ EVENTS

1. 6 December 1939: The Soviet 49th Rifle Division's 15th, 222nd and 212th Rifle regiments attack across the Taipale River.

2. 16–17 December 1939: The Soviet 49th and 150th Rifle divisions, supported by the 39th Light Tank Brigade and 240th Tank Battalion, launch a series of attacks on the Finnish defences, but are driven back.

3. In the early morning of 25 December 1939, elements of the 220th Rifle Regiment, 101st Rifle Regiment and 39th Rifle Regiment cross the frozen Lake Suvanto to establish bridgeheads at (north to south) Kelja, Volossula and Patoniemi.

4. Finnish counter-attacks destroy the Volossula and Patoniemi bridgeheads on 25 December 1939.

5. 26–27 December 1939: Three battalions of the 101st Rifle Regiment attack across Lake Suvanto in an attempt to consolidate the Kelja bridgehead. All attacks fail.

6. By evening of 27 December 1939, the Soviet bridgehead at Kelja has been reduced by Saarelainen's 6th Detached Battalion, assisted by Mueller's 3rd Battalion.

SOVIET OFFENSIVE IN THE TAIPALE SECTOR, 6–27 DECEMBER 1939

The Soviet attack took place in one of the harshest winters in years, with temperatures down to -20° C. The Soviets were attempting to open a route into southern Finland in the eastern Karelian Isthmus, but despite their superiority in numbers, they were initially unable to break through the Finnish defences.

N

40 ⊠
X X
BLICK

1

4 **8**

8

7

MANNERHEIM LINE

2

1

LAKE LADOGA

B

E

C

D

FINNISH
1. 40th Division (Blick)
2. 3rd Battalion, 29th Regiment (Mueller)
3. 6th Detached Battalion (Saarelainen)
4. 2nd Battalion, 30th Regiment (Sorri)
5. 1st Battalion, 30th Regiment (Sohlo)
6. 3rd Battalion, 30th Regiment
7. 23rd Regiment, 10th Division
8. Artillery

well and the Soviets secured footholds on the Koukkuniemi promontory. This allowed for the transfer of the remainder of the 49th Rifle Division to the promontory and also the crossing of the 150th Rifle Division, the 39th Light Tank Brigade and the 240th Detached (Flame-thrower) Tank Battalion. The crossing of these formations, under fire, seemed to herald a decisive action on the Finnish line. However, the Soviet attacks of 14–17 December were repulsed with heavy loss. On 14 December, after a heavy barrage that ceased at 1130hrs, Soviet tanks and infantry moved to the attack. Finnish artillery remained silent until the attack was well developed, despite the complaints of the infantry; it held its fire until both the Soviet tanks and their accompanying infantry had committed to it. Marching in almost parade-ground formations the Soviets moved forward, their tanks firing on the Finnish positions. When the Soviets had advanced into the kill zone that had been pre-registered for bombardment, the Finns opened a heavy and steady fire, their gunners methodically firing and reloading. In an artillery fire that was to become typical of the war, they used a mix of shrapnel bursts to cut down the infantry and also high-explosive rounds aimed at the tanks. The attacking Soviets bared up under this fire for about five minutes before retreating back to their own lines, often unable to retrieve their wounded. The attack cost them 300–400 killed and wounded and 18 tanks.

In an effort to relieve pressure on the formations on Koukkuniemi, elements of the 220th, 101st and 39th Rifle regiments crossed the frozen Lake Suvanto in the early hours of 25 December to establish bridgeheads at Kelja, Volossula and Patoniemi. The counter-attack by the Finnish 30th Infantry Regiment dislodged the Soviets from Volossula and Patoniemi later that day. In an attempt to support the troops caught in the Kelja bridgehead, three battalions of the 101st Rifle Regiment attacked across the ice on 26 and 27 December. All attacks failed, with none of these supporting troops making the shore at Kelja. By the end of 27 December, the final Soviet units at Kelja had been destroyed by the Finnish 6th Detached Battalion.

From the Soviet perspective, the Taipale offensive had been nothing short of a shambles. Massed infantry and tank attacks had achieved little gain but had resulted in huge casualties. In one attack, over 1,000 Soviet troops were killed while the armoured units lost 27 tanks. Despite advantages in materiel, command and control in attacks was poor, while artillery and air support faced significant difficulties in accurately targeting Finnish artillery and MG positions. In what was to become a characteristic feature of the war, the Finns had developed their positions to maximize terrain and water features and had expertly placed and concealed their support weapons. While Soviet troops had fully expected the Finns to break and run, they found that their opponents were dogged in defending prepared positions and they were also capable of mounting ferocious counter-attacks. For their part, as the Finns became more familiar with Soviet tanks, their expertise in dispatching

A posed photograph showing Finnish troops using a captured Soviet DP-27 light machine gun deployed in anti-aircraft mode. (SA-kuva)

them grew. As Finnish anti-tank guns were in short supply, they improvised other methods and used Molotovs, cluster grenades and satchel charges to destroy Soviet armour. In some cases, they even employed crowbars to damage the tracks on Soviet tanks.

As winter deepened on the Karelian Front, the attacks in the Taipale sector stalled. The planned northern envelopment of the Mannerheim Line by the Soviet 8th Army had also stalled in the Kollaa sector.

As the Finnish winter set in, and in temperatures that could drop as low as -40° C, the soldiers of the Soviet armies began to endure an icy martyrdom. Without suitable clothing and lacking the facilities to provide warm shelter and food on a consistent basis, thousands of soldiers would freeze to death, the result of poor planning and an overwhelming logistics gap.

And, as the offensives in the Taipale sector stalled, events further north were developing into one of the most significant and tragic episodes of the war along the Raate Road.

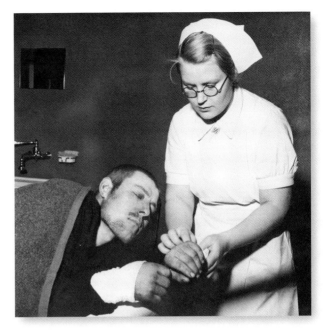

A Soviet prisoner of war receiving medical aid from a Finnish volunteer nurse, January 1940. Note the *Hakaristi* ('Cross of Freedom') swastika on the nurse's collar. (Keystone-France/Gamma-Keystone via Getty Images)

SUOMUSSALMI AND THE RAATE ROAD, 23 DECEMBER 1939–8 JANUARY 1940

In the central sector of the Finnish-Soviet frontier, the Soviet 9th Army had been tasked with attacking along a roughly east to west axis, their primary objective being the town of Oulu on the Gulf of Bothnia. The plan was to seize Oulu early in the campaign and thus cut Finland in two at its narrowest point. A key objective along this route of attack was the town of Suomussalmi, which sat on the junction of the southern Raate Road and also the road to Juntusranta. The 9th Army was commanded by Corps Commander Mikhail P. Dukhanov and consisted of four rifle divisions (44th, 122nd and 163rd Rifle divisions, and the 54th Mountain Rifle Division) plus one tank brigade. Together with its associated artillery, signals, logistics and NKVD detachments, the army numbered in excess of 50,000 troops. However, it had only been formed up as an army on 15 November and its component units had never trained or carried out exercises on a large scale together. There was very little sense of formation identity or cohesion within 9th Army. Furthermore, the terrain would dictate the plan of attack, and perhaps no other episode within the Winter War better demonstrates the challenges posed by the Finnish landscape. There were few roads in the area and there were only two main east to west routes: the northern Juntusranta Road and the southern Raate Road. This meant that the Soviet divisions advanced as long columns, strung out along the roads. Any mistakes in the order of the column could prove disastrous and, in the best-case scenario, the Soviets tried to advance with scout units and combat pioneers to the front of the column with tank and support weapons in close proximity. Subsequent

The reality of war. A frozen death was the ultimate end for many Soviet soldiers. Countless soldiers were to suffer this fate in the frozen wastes of the Finnish winter. (Keystone/Getty Images)

actions and the difficulties in crossing the various water obstacles in the sector resulted in this order being broken down. Logistics proved to be a constant problem, and it proved difficult to keep an entire column fed, fuelled and equipped with supplies of ammunition. The forest along the route usually extended to the road's edge, and this would later allow Finnish snipers and ambush patrols to approach close and unseen before unleashing an attack. In the heavily forested terrain, it proved next to impossible to use artillery and air support with any accuracy. Given the Finnish ability to move and attack in the winter terrain, the Soviet plan was rife for disaster. In the deepening winter, with temperatures plummeting to well below zero (-30° C was not uncommon), the Soviet force found it hard to maintain flank security as sentries naturally tended to return to the perceived safety and warmth of campfires within the column, especially at night.

In late November, the Soviet column began its advance with the 122nd Rifle Division moving towards Rovaniemi while the 163rd Rifle Division aimed for Puolanka, which lay at the halfway point between the border and Oulu. It would never reach this objective. Having attacked through the towns of Raate and Juntusranta, the 163rd Rifle Division advanced on Suomussalmi, which fell on 7 December. On 12 December, the 44th Rifle Division under Brigade Commander Aleksei I. Vinogradov began moving along the Raate Road in a westerly direction in order to support the 163rd's planned advance on Puolanka and thence to Oulu. In total, the 163rd and 44th Rifle divisions numbered around 15,000 troops.

To oppose them, the Finns had a composite force of border guards and Civil Guard detachments, bolstered by two detached regular battalions. These were reinforced by a task force that included the 27th Infantry Regiment under the command of Colonel Hjalmar Siilasvuo. Siilasvuo would prove to be an able commander and a master in unorthodox defensive tactics. Arriving at the Hyrynsalmi railhead on 8 December, Siilasvuo faced a seemingly deteriorating defensive situation with Suomussalmi in enemy hands and two Soviet divisions on the move in his direction. Having made a quick audit of available forces, which numbered around 11,000 including his task force and local units, he determined that his immediate priority was to prevent the 163rd Rifle Division and 44th Rifle Division from linking up on the Raate Road. On 11 December, Siilasvuo's task force launched its first counter-attack, cutting the Raate Road to the east of the 163rd Rifle Division and establishing a roadblock to prevent the 44th Rifle Division from linking up. The site for the roadblock

The remains of the village of Suomussalmi. The Finnish Army fought a decisive action in this sector from December 1939 to early January 1940, destroying the Soviet 163rd and 44th divisions. (Keystone-France/Gamma-Keystone via Getty Images)

was well chosen on a 1.5km strip of land, bordered at each end by a lake. These water features (lakes Kuivasjärvi and Kuomasjärvi) prevented a Soviet counter-attack at either flank of the roadblock. Ultimately, it was several days before elements of the 44th Rifle Division made contact at the roadblock, while the Soviet units at Suomussalmi (the 81st Mountain Rifle Regiment and the 759th Rifle Regiment) had been weakened in their advance and did not cooperate or coordinate their artillery to develop a counter-attack. Further away, Soviet tank units at Juntusranta lacked enough fuel to advance to the aid of either the 163rd or the 44th Rifle divisions. In the weeks that followed, the Finns developed a classic example of what is now known as a *motti* battle. A *motti* in Finnish refers to a cubic metre of firewood. Applied in this context, it referred to the tactic of deconstructing the Soviet columns into smaller, isolated units along the Raate Road. This allowed the Finns, despite their inferiority in numbers, to overwhelm sections of the divisional columns piece by piece. For the trapped Soviet units, it would mean slow, gradual destruction while, at the same time, they were challenged just to survive in the Finnish winter. The battles along the Raate Road illustrated the effectiveness of this tactic, and it was also employed on other Soviet columns during the campaign.

On 13 December, the Finns launched a series of raids along the road to contain the 44th Rifle Division, while putting in a focused attack on the 163rd Rifle Division. Reinforced with further troops to create what was now termed the 9th Division, Siilvasuo coordinated a series of attacks along the Raate Road, punishing both trapped divisions. Within the Soviet command there was some confusion. The 163rd Rifle Division's commander Andrei Zelentsov requested permission to withdraw, and was refused. Corps Commander Dukhanov seemed incapable of organizing a concerted and coordinated counter-attack, and was replaced on 22 December by Corps Commander Vasily I. Chuikov. This change in command did not improve the situation. Although only 9km separated the two Soviet divisions, a link-up proved to be impossible. On 27 December, the Finns launched a concerted

A Soviet pioneer unit in the early phase of the war. In this case, they are trying to remove some form of obstacle from their route. Such pioneer units found themselves increasingly challenged in the *motti* fighting that developed along the Raate Road. They found that the majority of road obstacles had been booby-trapped, while the approaches to them were also mined. Such tactics took a high toll among the pioneer units. (ullstein bild via Getty Images)

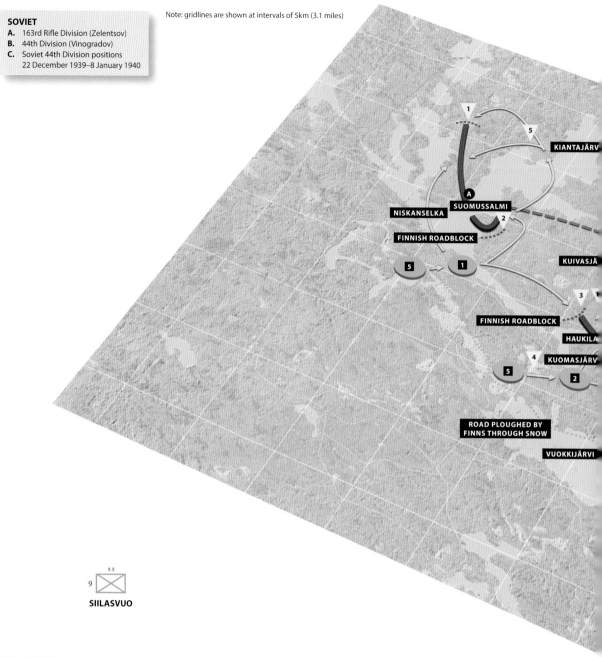

SOVIET
A. 163rd Rifle Division (Zelentsov)
B. 44th Division (Vinogradov)
C. Soviet 44th Division positions
    22 December 1939–8 January 1940

Note: gridlines are shown at intervals of 5km (3.1 miles)

KIANTAJÄRV

SUOMUSSALMI

NISKANSELKA

FINNISH ROADBLOCK

KUIVASJÄ

FINNISH ROADBLOCK

HAUKILA

KUOMASJÄRV

ROAD PLOUGHED BY
FINNS THROUGH SNOW

VUOKKIJÄRVI

9 ⟨× ×⟩
SIILASVUO

▼ EVENTS

1. By 11 December 1939, the Soviet 163rd Rifle Division, having pushed its lead elements across Kiantajärvi, has been halted at a Finnish roadblock created by elements of Siilvasuo's 9th Division.

2. The 163rd Rifle Division's rear elements also find the road blocked to their rear at Suomussalmi by Siilvasuo's men.

3. 11 December 1939: Elements of Battle Group Kontula block the advance of the Soviet 44th Division further to the east along the Raate Road, opening a gap between the Soviet 163rd and 44th divisions. This roadblock is reinforced between 23 and 29 December 1939.

4. 11 December 1939: Finnish units move into attack positions to the north and south of the Raate Road.

5. 27–30 December 1939: Finnish attacks strike the head, rear and flanks of the Soviet 163rd Rifle Division.

6. By 30 December 1939, the 163rd Rifle Division has been destroyed and surviving elements break up to retreat towards the Soviet border.

7. Finnish attacks also develop along the Soviet 44th Division positions to the east.

8. 1–2 January 1940: Finnish attacks develop at the westernmost edge of the Soviet 44th Division column near Haukila.

9. 2–4 January 1940: Finnish attacks are launched around the Kokkojärvi junction. This process has effectively cut the 44th Division column into *motti*.

10. 5 January 1940: Coordinated attacks at the head and rear of the 44th Division column by the four Finnish task forces.

11. The bridge at Purasjoki is cut by Finnish troops. Two Soviet regimental HQs are overrun.

12. 6–8 January 1940: Elements of the Soviet 44th Division attempt to break out through the forests. All other Soviet elements are destroyed along the Raate Road.

44

THE BATTLE OF SUOMUSSALMI/RAATE ROAD, 11 DECEMBER 1939–8 JANUARY 1940

The battle was a confusing action that took place across several phases of fighting. It was the most significant victory for Finnish forces in the north of the country, against superior Soviet forces.

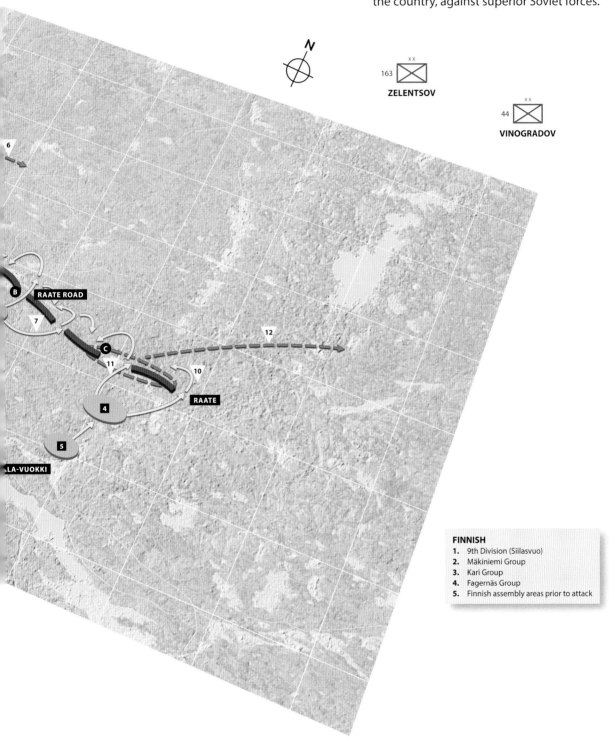

FINNISH
1. 9th Division (Siilasvuo)
2. Mäkiniemi Group
3. Kari Group
4. Fagernäs Group
5. Finnish assembly areas prior to attack

attack on the 163rd Rifle Division, forcing it out of Suomussalmi, after which it effectively disintegrated. Some elements of the division managed to escape across Lake Kiantajärvi while the 662nd Rifle Regiment was cut off and destroyed. By 30 December, the remnants of the 163rd Rifle Division had reached the Finnish-Soviet border. The Finns were now in a position to focus all of their attention on the 44th Rifle Division, which was strung out along 32km of the Raate Road and dug into defensive positions.

Starting during the night of 1/2 January 1940, Finnish forces began cutting the 44th Rifle Division column into *motti*, with attacks on the Raate Road near Haukila. Elements of 27th Infantry Regiment and 1st Guerrilla Battalion (Sissi P-1) under Captain Eino Lassila approached the Soviet column along a forest road to the south of Lake Kuivasjärvi under cover of darkness, using ahkio sleds to move ammunition and support weapons. Having established a base of fire using six heavy MGs and mortars as support, the Finns attacked the head of the column with a company on either side of the road. In theory, they were attacking strong Soviet elements, as there was both artillery and tanks at the western end of the 44th divisional column. However, the Finns found the Soviet soldiers huddled around fires and without their heavy weapons prepared for firing. In the fierce night fight that developed several Soviet units were annihilated, while a counter-attack with armoured cars was driven off with a pair of Finnish 37mm AT guns.

Survivors' accounts later described the fear and frustration of being trapped in a *motti*. The Finns moved invisibly in the forest while the Soviet sentries were picked off on a regular basis. Larger attacks could develop seemingly at a moment's notice. The attritive effects of fear, cold, hunger and battlefield stress eroded all unit cohesion and effective leadership. For some troops, the first Finns they actually saw were those who took them prisoner when their *motti*s collapsed. Hundreds of men tried to flee in small groups or individually through the forest in the direction of their own lines. It is unknown how many Soviet soldiers fled into the woods to try to escape and simply disappeared in the course of the various *motti* actions along the Finnish-Soviet frontier.

The attack of 1–2 January 1940 was a classic *motti* action, overwhelming a section of the road and destroying Soviet units on it; it created a 300–400m

The pity of war: casualties of the Soviet 44th Division strewn along the Raate Road. (Hulton-Deutsch Collection/CORBIS/Corbis via Getty Images)

gap in the column. The Finns repeated this exercise up and down the line, travelling parallel to the main road using skis and sleds and then attacking sections of the Soviet column. Between 2 and 4 January, there were further attacks by Task Force Kari around the Kokkojärvi road junction. Siilasvuo ordered an attack by his four task groups (Mandelin, Mäkkiniemi, Kari and Fagernäs) on 5 January, cutting the bridge at Purasjoki and overrunning the HQs of both the Soviet 25th and 146th Rifle regiments. The final collapse of the Soviet 44th Division was now close and, on 6 January, Vinogradov ordered a breakout attempt. Vinogradov and some elements of the 44th Rifle Division managed to retreat successfully to the border, but the remainder of the division was destroyed and had effectively ceased to exist by 8 January. Karl Mydans, a correspondent for *Time Life*, was given access to several parts of the front. He witnessed the aftermath of another *motti* action in the Salla sector and admitted that, for the assembled war reporters, it was the most horrible sight that they had ever seen. It is worth bearing in mind that many of these reporters had covered the Spanish Civil War. For a distance of many kilometres, Soviet Ford trucks lay burnt out, abandoned and often riddled with bullets. Pathetically, all of the destroyed vehicles were orientated towards Finland. The debris of the column lay everywhere – discarded food supplies, clothing, shoes, weapons and ammunition of all types. Worst of all for the reporters were the hundreds of dead Soviet soldiers and horses, frozen all along the road, with the snow stained pink with blood (Mydans 1959, p. 19.) Surveying this devastation, Mydans reported that one of the Finnish officers remarked: 'The wolves will eat well this year.'

American war correspondent Carl Mydans in the field in January 1940. The 'David and Goliath' nature of the conflict, and the general inactivity of the 'Phoney War' in Europe, resulted in many war correspondents relocating to Finland. (Photo by Carl Mydans/ The LIFE Picture Collection via Getty Images)

By any measure, the Suomussalmi and Raate Road battles had been an astonishing victory for the Finns. In particular, the Soviet 44th Rifle Division had disintegrated in spectacular fashion, leaving most of its heavy equipment and transport abandoned on the Raate Road. This was something that the Finns immediately capitalized upon, and reporters were allowed to photograph the bleak scenes of destruction. In all, the Soviets had lost 43 tanks, ten armoured cars, over 260 trucks and vast amounts of other military equipment including rifles, MGs, artillery, anti-tank guns and much-prized radio and telephone sets. The number of Soviet losses is still debated and modern estimates range from 22,000 to over 27,000. This was compared to Finnish losses of around 2,700.

Such statistics cannot illustrate the horrendous experience of the Soviet soldiers caught in the *motti*. The mere act of surviving the winter conditions was challenging enough and many soldiers simply froze to death. With fuel in short supply, tanks and vehicles were immobilized, while field kitchens were targeted and the men faced starvation. Efforts to resupply the columns from the air proved to be courageous but largely ineffective. In the midst of this, Finnish troops seemed to be able to move at will and emerge to conduct hit-and-run raids or more concentrated attacks. Finnish snipers, nicknamed by the Soviets as 'cuckoos', targeted officers and NCOs and gradually developed a slow attrition within regimental and battalion leadership.

ATTACK ON THE SOVIET 44TH DIVISION, RAATE ROAD, 1 JANUARY 1940 (PP. 48–49)

In the *motti* actions that typified this war, the Finns used the mobility provided by skis to great advantage. For the immobilized column of the Soviet 44th Division (**1**) shown here, the New Year opened with a night-time attack by Finnish ski parties. The raiding Finnish parties have established themselves along both sides of the road in order to be able to fire down its axis.

Such Finnish ski parties usually carried a high number of Suomi SMGs (**2**) and these were highly effective when used in numbers at short distances. In this way the Finns inflicted high casualties among the Soviet troops huddled around campfires by the roadside. In their rucksacks (**3**) the Finns carried grenades and Molotov cocktails, which they used with some effect on the vehicles stacked up along the road. In their approach to the

attack, they used their *puukko* knives (**4**) to silence Soviet sentries. Once the attack was well underway on both sides of the road, Finnish soldiers would, individually or in groups, place demolition charges (**5**) in nearby vehicles and tanks. The cumulative battlefield effect was total mayhem along an entire section of the Soviet column.

In this case, the attack was a fleeting one, but the Finns would return with larger parties to create 300–400m gaps in the column. They also showed a capacity to build substantial roadblocks to create such gaps and to trap Soviet troops in *motti*. These roadblocks were often constructed while under fire. The actions along the Raate Road were a prime example of these tactics, but they would be repeated on various locations along the Finnish-Soviet frontier.

The psychological burden on Soviet troops trapped in *motti*s can scarcely be imagined. On a nightly basis, sentries were dispatched by gun or knife at the perimeters of the column. Alternatively, Finnish troops infiltrated past the sentries to silently kill soldiers huddled within the column. As grim practical jokes, dead Soviet soldiers who had frozen solid were propped up as signposts along the route. In every respect, the Soviet attack on the Central Finland sector had proved to be a costly and humiliating defeat. It is perhaps unsurprising that Brigade Commander Vinogradov, having escaped from the *motti* and returned to Soviet lines, was court-martialled on 11 January and later executed along with other members of his staff.

Finnish ski troops deploying in ambush, January 1940. (SA-kuva)

THE BATTLE OF TOLVAJÄRVI, 12 DECEMBER 1939

This battle on the Ladoga Karelia front was the first offensive victory for the Finns during the war. While they were enjoying a level of success along the entire front, this was usually in a defensive posture. The battlefield was to the north of Lake Ladoga and, as both sides prepared their offensive moves, they planned to cross the frozen lakes in the region. These included lakes Hirvasjärvi and Tolvajärvi.

On the Soviet side, the 139th Rifle Division commanded by Brigade Commander Nikolai Beljalev consisted of the 364th, 609th and 718th Rifle regiments supported by around 30 tanks and over 300 aircraft. In total there were over 20,000 Soviet troops in the sector, and they were tasked with pushing westwards to secure the Lieksa–Joensu–Pyhäselka road. Their initial objective was the village of Tolvajärvi. The fact that the Soviet units were moving forward to the attack as the Finns began their own assault created considerable operational difficulties for the Finns.

On the Finnish side, there were just over 4,000 troops available, formed up in 16th Infantry Regiment and the ad hoc composite groups of the Talvela Group (from IV Corps) and the Rjasjanen Detachment (four infantry battalions and one artillery battalion).[6] In total, the Finns had seven under-strength infantry battalions and one artillery battalion. On the positive side, they also had some of the ablest commanders of the war in this sector. Foremost among these was Colonel Paavo Talvela, commander of Group Talvela. He was an officer of considerable experience and had served in the Jäger battalion during World War I and the Civil War. Perhaps most importantly in this context, during his general staff course Talvela had written a thesis on how to counter just such an attack. He did this in collaboration with Lieutenant-Colonel Aaro Pajari, who now was appointed to command 16th Infantry Regiment in the sector. So, the senior commander in the sector

---

6   Among 16th Infantry Regiment was a reserve unit from Tampere, commanded by the local police chief.

A Finnish soldier man-hauling a machine gun on a sled. The Finns showed themselves to be masters at using relatively simple equipment to increase their combat mobility. (Keystone-France/Gamma-Keystone via Getty Images)

and one of his most important subordinates had theorized at some length on how to counter exactly the type of attack that the Soviets were now developing. In the face of a number of reverses along the line, Talvela realized that the army and the whole nation needed a morale boost. With Pajari, he developed a scheme for an offensive which, considering the numerical superiority of the Soviets to his front, was daring if not downright foolhardy. Their plan now was to initiate quite an elaborate pincer movement, with two wings of the Finnish forces crossing the frozen Hirvasjärvi and Tolvajärvi lakes. This offensive would start on 12 December 1939, but was preceded by a large-scale raid during the night of 8/9 December. Two parties of Finns bypassed the Soviet front line and piquets, and penetrated into the Soviet rear area. One group of Finns had to turn back due to encountering an impassable water obstacle, but the other party pressed on. Under the personal command of Pajari, they dispatched enemy troops with their *puukko* knives en route. Near the Kivisalmi Bridge, they found themselves overlooking the camps of three Soviet battalions and, by firing on each battalion in turn from different locations, they got the three enemy battalions firing at each other. The Finns then exfiltrated out of the area while the Soviet battalions continued firing at each other for another three hours. On his way back, Pajari collapsed with a mild heart attack.[7]

Lead elements of the Soviet 718th Rifle Regiment reached Tolvajärvi village on 10 December after a five-day forced march. Having pushed back the Finnish defenders, they were on the verge of encircling the Finnish positions and capturing both artillery and supply elements when they captured the field kitchens. Exhausted and starving, the troops began to feast on the hot sausage stew that had just been prepared. Cobbling together two composite companies of rear-echelon troops (cooks, clerks and staff officers), Pajari put in a counter-attack that night, and in the bitter hand-to-hand fight that

7 Pajari had a heart condition that he had concealed from Talvela and his men. Despite this, he continued to serve for the remainder of the Winter War and would serve in the later Continuation and Lapland wars. He died of a sudden heart attack, on his way to work, in 1949.

followed the Soviet advance was stopped. The episode would later become known as 'the Sausage War'.

On 12 December, the Finnish forces began their offensive at 0800hrs and Pajari would again be in tactical command (Talvela had wanted to lead himself but was dissuaded by officers on his staff). Their forces had now been split into three groups. A two-battalion Task Force M (commanded by Major Jaakko Malkamäki) would attack to the north side of Tolvajärvi village. Once Task Force M was fully engaged, Pajari would lead a three-battalion force across the frozen Hirvasjärvi lake towards objectives on Kotisaari Island. A further force of over two battalions under Major Erik Paloheimo would act as force reserve.

The northern wing of the Finnish attack, comprising Task Force M, initially fared well. Mistaken by Soviet troops as friendly forces, they advanced until they met the disorganized battalions of the Soviet 718th Rifle Regiment, overrunning its command post and mortally wounding its commander. Thereafter, Soviet resistance stiffened and Major Malkamäki ordered his task force back to its original jump-off area.

The main effort under Pajari made better going, despite their start time being delayed. Supported by artillery and MGs in battery, they advanced on Kotisaari Island. Due to the withdrawal of Task Force M, Pajari's forces found themselves operating largely alone. There was fierce resistance at Kotisaari Island, which developed into a battle within the battle. The attacking forces were eventually supported by four further Finnish companies before overrunning the island and taking 60 Soviet POWs and capturing a number of artillery pieces.

The Soviets also had a strongpoint in a hotel on the eastern shore of Lake Tolvajärvi, which was set within defensive positions and supported by MGs, mortars and artillery. The fight here went on till around 1430hrs, with the Finns putting in a number of attacks on this strong position. This action ended with grim, short-range exchanges within the hotel and hand-to-hand action. For a loss of around 100 killed and some 250 wounded, the Finns had inflicted a loss of around 1,000 casualties (some estimates put this figure as high as 5,000) on the Soviets. Furthermore, they had overrun a weapons depot to the east of the hotel position and captured artillery pieces, including AT guns, over 60 heavy MGs and 20 armoured vehicles, including T-26 tanks. This equipment, in itself, provided a significant boost for the Finnish war effort. Within the hotel, the Finns discovered Soviet communications and HQ files.

Despite the setbacks associated with Task Force M, the attack had been a success and Pajari had displayed an ability to organize attacks in different directions as the engagement progressed. The move had also thwarted the plans of the Soviet force to continue its own offensive to the east. Talvela wanted to press forward again that day but, in light of the exhaustion of the troops and the disorganization after the attack, Pajari persuaded him to stand down. This was undoubtedly wise, as the Finnish officer and NCO cohort had suffered serious losses within the otherwise small Finnish death toll. However,

Soviet prisoners of war smile for the camera. (SA-kuva)

VILLAGE DEFENCE, LADOGA KARELIA SECTOR, DECEMBER 1939 (PP. 54–55)

In this early phase of the war, Soviet troops had not yet learned the dangers of advancing into seemingly quiet Finnish border villages. Here, the Soviet troops (**1**) are advancing in extended order and one has already triggered an anti-personnel mine. They would soon learn that all approaches to such locations, both roads and roadsides, would most likely be mined. The tanks in support are also about to be targeted by the ambush party. In this case, the Suomi gunner (**2**) has initiated the ambush once the tanks have moved closer to the village. All other Finnish soldiers would then join in to provide suppressing fire for the tank demolition party (**3**) to close in on the tanks. This Finnish soldier will use a cluster charge, but Molotov cocktails and satchel charges were also used. Finnish

soldiers have also been placed in and on the surrounding buildings (**4**). In a relatively short time, the Soviets would realize that any village buildings left standing (**5**) would most like be booby-trapped.

Soon, all Soviet advances were covered by combat pioneers so that routes into villages and towns could be cleared of mines. Such troops suffered a disproportionally high casualty rate. Even in towns that had been deliberately destroyed during the Finnish withdrawal booby-traps might be hidden. In some cases, these were placed in the context of dead livestock in an effort to catch out hungry soldiers. As winter deepened, the Finns donned snow overalls to blend in and disappear, further compounding the difficulties of the Soviets.

Part of the Finnish Army headquarters in flames, Mikkeli, January 1940. Deliberate demolitions were employed in order to deny the enemy cover and shelter. In many cases, buildings that were left standing were booby-trapped by the retreating Finns. (SA-kuva)

for the embattled Finnish nation, the success at Tolvajärvi came as a much-needed boost for morale.

Fighting was renewed in this sector and, up until 22 December, a battle raged for the village of Ägläjärvi. Having pushed on to the Aittojoki River, the Finns set up defensive positions and thereafter this became a quiet sector on the line. During the battle for Ägläjärvi, Soviet statistics indicate that they lost 6,490 soldiers in the area – killed, wounded and missing. These included the commander of the 75th Rifle Division, Brigade Commander Aleksander Stepanov, who was wounded. Finnish losses were considerably less with a total of 748 – killed, wounded and missing. But it is worth bearing in mind that Finnish manpower was finite. Such losses could not be replaced and also represented a heavy toll in the context of the small population of Finland. In the aftermath of the Tolvajärvi fighting, Talvela was promoted to major-general while Pajari became a full colonel. Towards the end of the war, Talvela was appointed to command III Corps on the Karelian Isthmus.

THE KOLLAA SECTOR, 7 DECEMBER 1939–13 MARCH 1940

In contrast to these dramatic actions in the Ladoga Karelia sector, the war in the Kollaa sector was often inactive but was also punctuated with phases of intense action. On 7 December, the Soviet 56th Division (8th Army) had pushed towards the Kollaa River and the local Finnish forces fell back around 40km under intense artillery fire and tank attacks. This was seen as a key sector as a Soviet success here would compromise the entire Finnish IV Corps and then allow them to sweep southwards to attack the Mannerheim Line defences from the rear. It became imperative for the Finns to hold a line on the Kollaa River. During the initial days of the attack, the Finns worked hard to improve their defences and trenches; this was a difficult undertaking as the ground was frozen hard. The sector was

A patrol of the 6th Company, 34th Infantry Regiment at Suojärvi in December 1939. Facing the camera is Private Juha Aho. The total exhaustion of these troops is immediately apparent. The 34th Infantry Regiment was tasked with delaying the seemingly overwhelming Soviet numbers in this sector. (SA-kuva)

the defensive responsibility of Major-General Woldemar Hägglund's 12th Division. By 17 December, the attacks of the Soviet 8th Army had stalled totally and Stavka ordered its forces to dig in. The front later became so quiet that some Finnish forces were diverted to help in the destruction of a *motti* at Uomaa.

Finnish troops in a heated bunker. Throughout the war, the Finnish Army displayed an ability to provide warm bunkers and tents, which allowed its troops to remain effective even in the worst of the winter weather. This contrasted hugely with Soviet capabilities in this respect; the Red Army often could not provide its men with adequate food and shelter as they advanced into Finland. (Keystone-France/Gamma-Keystone via Getty Images)

The war in this sector became largely attritional, with the Soviets subjecting the Finnish lines to heavy bombardments. The Finns held some advantages, however, as there were few roads in the area and this allowed them to focus their defence. It was here also that Simo Häyhä established his reputation as the deadliest sniper of all time. Yet, as the campaign wore on and the Finnish losses mounted, the Soviets were reinforcing their formations in the sector. As the Finns came under increasing pressure in Karelia, the pressure on the Kollaa front intensified. A massive Soviet attack in January 1940 led to the Battle of Killer Hill – a desperate defence by 32 Finns of an entrenched hill position. Faced by over 4,000 Soviet troops, the Finns inflicted a loss of over 400 on the attacking enemy before the position was taken. Only four Finns survived the fight. On 2 March, the Soviets began a new offensive and a to-and-fro fight developed, with the Soviets taking several positions only to be later driven out by Finnish counter-attacks. Having suffered great loss, the Soviet 56th Division managed to cross the Kollaa River on 7 March. In the final days of the war, there was intense fighting as the Soviets pushed to extend this bridgehead. Despite the intensity of the fighting, the majority of the Kollaa sector remained in Finnish hands at the ceasefire.

Officers of the 69th Jäger Regiment in the Kollaa River sector in March 1940. The strain of continuous combat is obvious. They are, left to right, Lieutenant Leinonen, Captain Suna and Reserve Lieutenant Laine. (SA-kuva)

The fighting here also gave rise to the key phrase of Finnish resistance in the war. At a particularly difficult time in the fighting, Major-General Hägglund asked, 'Will Kollaa hold?' The answer was supplied by Lieutenant Aarne Juutilainen, a former legionnaire in the French Foreign Legion and a tenacious fighter, who responded: 'Kollaa holds' ('*Kollaa Kestää*'). The phrase has entered the Finnish lexicon and is associated with concepts of resistance, determination and *sisu*.

THE DEVELOPMENT OF FINNISH TACTICS

It is worth taking a moment to consider how Finnish tactics developed from late November 1939. In essence, the army and its associated reservists, Civil Guard and border guard contingents had been trained along conventional lines. However, there was a level of flexibility in the training programmes that allowed for battlefield innovation. Married to this was the Finns' innate capacities for improvisation as well as excellent field skills. Across the army, there were good levels of marksmanship and this fed into the mystique of the Finnish infantry as snipers. It is obvious that there were far fewer actual snipers deployed than the Soviets later reported. The Finns were generally just good shots and were excellent at concealment. The average infantryman had the capacity to engage in some level of sniping and this acted as a force multiplier across the army. The Finnish sniper Simo Häyhä, known as the 'White Death', is the best-known sniper from the Winter War. Operating in the Kollaa sector he reached a score of confirmed kills measured in the hundreds. But across all fronts the Finns fielded large numbers of snipers,

The legendary Finnish sniper Simo Häyäh. Credited with over 500 confirmed kills, he used the Finnish M28/30 rifle, a version of the Mosin-Nagant, and also the Suomi SMG; both of which he fired over iron sights. He usually worked alone without a spotter. Badly wounded in March 1940 when he was hit in the face by an explosive bullet, he nevertheless survived the war and died in 2002. (SA-kuva)

who showed excellent marksmanship and field skills in their attacks on Soviet units. Few were armed with scoped rifles, but many such rifles were captured and put to good use in the Winter War and the later Continuation War. Many soldiers, including Simo Häyhä, also used the Suomi SMG and even the Lahti M-26 as sniping weapons. The use of the Suomi in this fashion necessitated a careful stalk close to the enemy or the setting of an ambush. But many a Soviet soldier fell to a sniping attack from this weapon.

There were aspects of the Suomi SMG that also emphasized its use as a support weapon. In such cases, a Suomi gunner and a loader could lay down supporting or suppressing fire over short ranges. Despite the low numbers of this weapon within the army, it had a significant impact and facilitated attacks on *motti* in which the Finns could ski close to a convoy before opening a short but devastating volley of SMG fire.

From the early stages of the war, the Finns had also engaged in booby-trapping operations. These tactics included the mining of roads, mining barricades on roads and also along routes of approach. If the Soviets found a house still standing as they advanced, they learned through bitter experience to expect booby-traps. Within a house, these could include underfloor devices initiated by

Finnish troops wire-cutting during an operation in February 1940, showing the signs of having campaigned through the winter. Although quite basic, their snow suits provided good protection and camouflage. (Picture Post/ Hulton Archive/Getty Images)

pressure triggers and booby-trapped cupboards and stoves. The Finns also showed an uncanny ability to recognize areas where Soviet troops might take cover after a booby-trap or mortar attack. These areas would be mined to inflict a follow-up attack on troops seeking cover.

Throughout the war, the Finns showed a marked ability to develop their defence. Terrain was usually well picked in order to maximize the use of high ground or, as in some cases in Karelia, in order to force the Soviets to attack over open spaces. Trench lines were usually constructed within forested areas, making them hard to spot and target. The Finns were expert in factoring water features, which are present in abundance in Finland, into their defensive plans. Lakes, rivers and marshes quite often formed part of the Finnish line, protecting flanks when defending against Soviet attacks. Artillery guns and shells were in short supply, so barrages were short and focused and, where possible, efforts were made to pre-range in on possible routes of advance. Finnish maps were excellent and the gunners showed remarkable skill in utilizing their geographical knowledge. As always, the infantry complained of a lack of artillery support, but this was largely down to the lack of materiel. Heavy MGs were available in numbers and these were used to great effect in defence and were often deployed in battery fire. At the same time, efforts were made to move

A booby-trap device attached to a tree. Set at head or shoulder height in a forest, such devices posed a serious threat to an unwary patrol. The Finns showed considerable aptitude in developing and deploying such devices from early in the war. Soviet engineer units also became more proficient in booby-trapping and mining as the war progressed. (SA-kuva)

A Finnish Bofors AA position. The Finns possessed too few of these guns to mount a comprehensive defence on all fronts, but they still enjoyed some success. (SA-kuva)

up support weapons, such as heavy MGs and mortars, in support of infantry attacks. This was often achieved by man-hauling the weapons – with sleds in snow conditions, and even the use of reindeer.

The highly effective Bofors 37mm AT gun was in short supply and in some cases these weapons were moved around the front as required at considerable effort. When available, they could have a deadly effect on the Soviet tanks, and the Finnish AT gunners quickly learned to hold their fire until a tank was trying to clear an obstacle and thus exposing its lightly armoured underside. The relative dearth of such weapons also necessitated a level of invention in terms of anti-tank tactics. Having been initially panicked by the appearance of Soviet tanks, the Finnish infantry quickly realized that without their supporting infantry, they were highly vulnerable. Dedicated tank-killing squads attacked the Soviets using cluster grenades, Molotovs, satchel charges and other improvised devices. In some cases, Finnish troops threw burning petrol-soaked blankets over forward vision ports before moving in to a dispatch tank. There were also instances where crowbars were employed to damage tracks on stationary tanks. It is interesting that such tactics were widely reported in the press and would later be used by tank-killing units within various armies during World War II.

While excellent in defence, ambush and unconventional operations, major Finnish offensives were not without problems. The Finns showed themselves to be excellent in counter-attack, but some of their offensives in Karelia and the Kollaa sectors fared less well. Due to the lack of communications equipment and staff training among officers, offensive plans were sometimes underdeveloped. Coordinating moves to start lines and artillery cooperation proved difficult. There was a further reality at play in that the Finns simply did not have the numbers to overwhelm Soviet formations in an attack. Inventive defence was one thing, but the assets for a decisive attack were frequently beyond them.

In organizational terms, the Finnish success in the use of composite and ad hoc units was notable. Throughout the war, task forces and battle groups were organized under local commanders. To war correspondents

Finnish troops with a wrecked Soviet T-26 tank. At the beginning of the war, the Finns had been overawed at the appearance of Soviet armour on the battlefield. They soon developed a range of methods of dispatching them, from the use of AT guns to the deployment of tank-killing sections armed with cluster grenades and satchel bombs. (SA-kuva)

covering the war, this often looked like an act of desperation. However, these mixed units of regulars, reservists, Civil Guard and border units generally performed well beyond expectation. The success was rooted in effective pre-war training programmes. Throughout World War II, the various belligerent nations would field similar-style ad hoc formations, particularly the Germans.

As an example of a military achieving tactical success based on relatively meagre assets, the Finnish example in the Winter War has provided some useful 'lessons learned' in the past. This held true during the Cold War when NATO armies considered how best to slow the Soviet Bloc juggernaut with forces that were, numerically at least, inferior. In more recent times, with militaries across the globe being asked to be more effective while using fewer resources of all kinds, the Winter War still offers useful lessons.

An ad hoc Finnish sauna located near the front. It was perhaps one of the more bizarre elements of this conflict that, while Soviet troops struggled to survive, their Finnish counterparts contrived to construct field saunas. (SA-kuva)

PETSAMO AND LAPLAND, 1939–40

In the context of achieving set objectives, the campaign in the far north of Finland was an unqualified Soviet success. The Soviet 14th Army, commanded by Corps Commander Valerian A. Frolov, was tasked with seizing the port of Petsamo, Finland's only port on the Arctic Sea, and then exploiting as far south as possible. The 14th Army was also set the strategic peninsula of Rybachi as a key objective. In total Frolov had over 52,000 troops at his disposal in the 14th, 52nd and 104th divisions, and in the initial action he would deploy two of these divisions (52nd and 104th) assisted by the Soviet Northern Fleet. Apart from denying the Finns access to the Arctic Sea, the Soviets wished to capture local nickel mines while also establishing a presence that would deter any foreign intervention forces landing at Petsamo.

The area fell within the defensive remit of the Finnish Lapland Group (part of the North Finland Group), commanded by Major-General Martti Wallenius. A colourful character to say the least, Wallenius was a former Jäger who had been implicated in the kidnapping of President Kaarlo Stahlberg and took part in the Mäntsälä Rebellion, serving a year in prison for the latter. However, his fighting qualities could not be ignored, and he was recalled to the reserves at the start of the war before being given command of the Lapland Group in December 1939. Wallenius had only a composite unit of less than battalion strength (around 900 troops) on location to meet the initial Soviet landings. Commanded by Captain Antti Pennanen, this small task force of infantry, artillery and reconnaissance troops would conduct the defence until supported by other units from the Lapland Group.

The Soviet operation of 30 November was carried out with little difficulty. Landed from boats of the Northern Fleet, units of the 104th Division took the Rybachi Peninsula and Parkkina while the 52nd Division seized Petsamo. Task Force Pennanen fought a series of rearguard actions, but despite their

Military operations, December 1939–January 1940

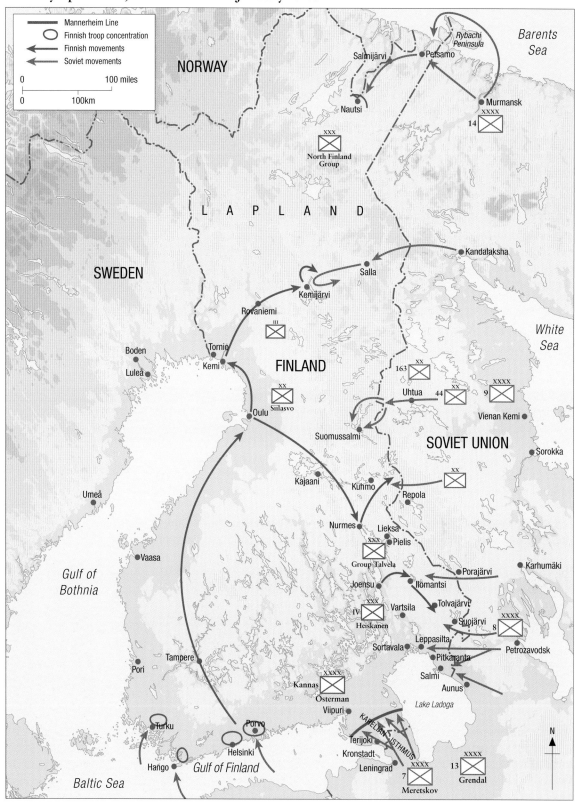

Legend:
- Mannerheim Line
- Finnish troop concentration
- Finnish movements
- Soviet movements

0 — 100 miles
0 — 100km

NORWAY

Barents Sea

Rybachi Peninsula

Salmijärvi

Petsamo

Nautsi

Murmansk

XXXX
14

North Finland Group
XXX

LAPLAND

Kandalaksha

Salla

Kemijärvi

Rovaniemi

III

SWEDEN

White Sea

Boden

Tornio

Kemi

Luleå

FINLAND

Siilasvo
XX

Oulu

163
XX

Uhtua

44
XX

9
XXXX

Vienan Kemi

Suomussalmi

SOVIET UNION

Sorokka

Umeå

Kajaani

Kuhmo

Repola

XX

Nurmes

Lieksa

Pielis

Group Talvela
XXX

Porajärvi

Karhumäki

Vaasa

Joensu

Ilomantsi

Tolvajärvi

Suojärvi

8
XXXX

Gulf of Bothnia

IV
XXX

Heiskanen

Vartsila

Sortavala

Leppasilta

Pitkaranta

Petrozavodsk

Tampere

Salmi

Aunus

Pori

Kannas
XXXX

Österman

Viipuri

Lake Ladoga

Turku

Porvo

KARELIAN ISTHMUS

N

Hango

Helsinki

Gulf of Finland

Terijoki

Kronstadt

Leningrad

7
XXXX

Meretskov

13
XXXX

Grendal

Baltic Sea

64

Soviet troops in attack, early 1940. This is often captioned as an action in the Winter War. It could also be one of the elaborate rehearsals undertaken by the Red Army in the run-up to the March offensives. This might explain the presence of a cameraman so close to the action. (Sovfoto/Universal Images Group via Getty Images)

best efforts were gradually dislodged and pushed southwards. The Soviets now intended to take Rovaniemi, the capital of Lapland, and push on to the Arctic Highway in order to cut off Finnish troops to the north. The Finns gathered together about four battalions in order to stop them, and a key action took place at the Kitinen bridgehead on 17/18 December. After an intense fight between the Soviet 273rd Mountain Rifle Regiment and two battalions of the Finnish 40th Infantry Regiment, the Finns began to fall back due to the appearance of two Soviet tanks. However, another Finnish unit struck at the Soviet supply columns and artillery positions in the rear, causing panic among the Soviet troops. The Soviets fled, leaving much equipment strewn on the battlefield. Wallenius then employed *motti* tactics against the 273rd Rifle Regiment in an action now known as the Battle of Pelkosenniemi (17–19 December), and it is claimed that he was the first to do so. This resulted in the virtual destruction of the three battalions of the 273rd Rifle Regiment, and the survivors fled northwards. So exhausted were the Finnish troops that they

Swedish volunteers manning a Maxim machine gun in January 1940. (Keystone-France/Gamma-Keystone via Getty Images)

could not pursue, and contact was broken until 21 December when Soviet forces were confirmed as being at Savukoski. At this point, the front line became static for almost two months. The plummeting winter temperatures and the days of almost total darkness restricted Soviet movements. The Finns were content to engage in guerrilla-style raiding in the Soviet rear area – destroying vehicles, cutting phone lines and killing sentries. For the average Soviet soldier, it was a freezing, black, nightmare existence.

There was some bitter fighting between the Lapland Group and Soviet forces in the vicinity of Lake Joutsijärvi and positions around Moitavaara. The 88th Rifle Division was ordered from Archangel to reinforce, but in mid-January 1940, Stavka ordered a withdrawal to new positions around Lake Märkäjärvi. On 26 January 1940, the Task Force SFK (*Svenska frivilligkaren* – Swedish Volunteer Corps), made up of Swedish and Norwegian volunteers and supported by six Swedish fighter planes and four bombers of the volunteer aviation group, took over responsibility for the Lapland sector. Thereafter the sector remained largely quiet, with the Swedish task force losing just 70 men in action.

Having taken its objectives early in the campaign, the Soviet 14th Army was then effectively contained. The Finns managed to keep them away from any further useful objectives, and the harshness of the climate during winter further curtailed movement. Between late February and the ceasefire, there was some further, although limited action, but overall this was a case study in the containment of a larger force.[8]

TANK BATTLE AT HONKANIEMI, KARELIAN ISTHMUS, 26 FEBRUARY 1940

While there were literally thousands of tanks deployed during the Winter War by the Soviets, there was virtually no armour opposition from the Finns. The Finnish Army had not invested in armour during the 1920s and 1930s and this was largely due to budgetary constraints. There were also practical issues and there was much discussion within the Finnish military as to the usefulness of tanks in the context of the terrain. In some areas, there was quite a limited road network and there were extensive natural obstacles in the shape of lakes, rivers, marshes and forested zones. At the outbreak of the war, the Finns had some obsolete Renault FT-17s and a small number of Vickers Mark E 6-ton tanks. Thirteen of the Vickers tanks were grouped in the 4th Company of the Finnish Armoured Battalion. Due to their scarcity, the Finns had been miserly in the deployment of their tanks, but the 4th Company was assigned to assist in the attack at Honkaniemi.

The location of Honkaniemi was to the south-east of Viipuri. Here the Soviets had advanced on an uneven front and created a salient for themselves. The Soviet left flank was covered by Lake Näjkkijärvi, but the commander of the Finnish II Corps, Lieutenant-General Harald Öhquist, and his 23rd Division commander (Colonel Voldemar Oinonen) saw an opportunity to pinch off this salient and perhaps trap Soviet forces against the lake. The local Finnish forces were from the 23rd Division and were reinforced by elements of 3rd Jäger Battalion and the 4th Company of the Armoured

---

8 Major-General Wallenius was transferred south to assist in the defence of Viipuri in February 1940, but showing the strain of combat and engaging in heavy drinking, he was relieved a few days later.

The Karelian Isthmus, January–February 1940

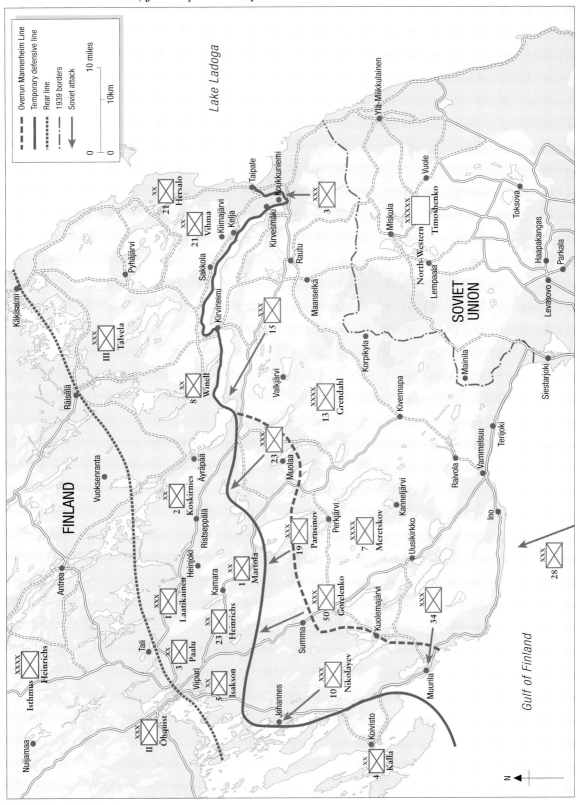

Battalion. Colonel Oinonen also succeeded in securing the return of the 67th Infantry Regiment which had been on loan to another division. The final Finnish order of battle would include four infantry battalions, two artillery battalions and the armoured company.

They were opposed by the Soviet 84th Rifle Division, which was supported by 35th Light Tank Brigade and the 112th Independent Tank Battalion. The Soviet tanks included large numbers of the T-26 tank, which was itself a development of the British Vickers 6-tonner. In the tank engagement that developed, therefore, there was a clash of tanks of almost identical type. The Finns planned to start their attack at 0500hrs on 26 February but this time was then set back to 0615hrs. Coincidentally, the Soviet forces were also planning an attack that day, scheduled to start at 1200hrs. As the Finns opened their attack, they found that the Soviets were also in the process of organizing themselves at their start lines, so the enemy was fully prepared.

The initial Finnish deployment started well with the Jäger units being carried by truck to Heponotko and from there they skied to their start line near Honkaniemi, arriving there around 0400hrs. Thereafter the plan began to hit a succession of glitches. While moving to the start line, five of the 13 Vickers tanks broke down. Then, due to confused communication over start times and start lines, there was a 'friendly fire' artillery incident that killed or wounded 30 Finnish soldiers. This put the start time back further.

After a short artillery bombardment by batteries of the 5th and 21st Artillery battalions, the attack finally got underway. A further two tanks broke down at the start line, leaving the Finns with just six to support the advance of the Jäger units. For the infantry, the attack was a difficult one. On the Finnish right flank, the attack stalled in the face of murderous Soviet firepower. The 2nd and 3rd Jäger companies advanced as far as the rail line on the left flank before they, too, were halted by heavy fire.

This only left the six Finnish tanks, under the command of Captain Ilmari Kunnas (3rd Jäger Battalion), in the battle. Coordination of the attack was difficult due to the lack of radios in the Vickers tanks, but they put up a

A Soviet section in attack in Finland, 1940. This could well be a staged propaganda photograph, but it shows the use of the LMG crew as fire support. By 1940, the aimless, massed advances of Soviet troops were a thing of the past. (Keystone-France\Gamma-Rapho via Getty Images)

plucky fight in face of the Soviet tank units, commanded by Colonel V. Kashuba.[9] Throughout the action it proved difficult to get the Jäger troops to support the tanks, and a 37mm AT gun assigned to the infantry does not seem to have destroyed any Soviet tanks.

One Finnish tank became stuck in a ditch and, with a damaged turret, this tank later returned to its jump-off point. The tank of Lieutenant Väinö Mikkola advanced the furthest into Soviet lines, penetrating to a distance of 500m before being knocked out. A further tank got bogged down, while the remaining four were also knocked out by Soviet T-26s and AT guns. It was a short, sharp fight with both sides registering hits on enemy tanks. The tank of Corporal E. Seppälä continued to engage targets after being immobilized. The Soviet official report noted that the six Finnish tanks had been put out of action by three of their T-26s. Many of the Finnish crewmen, having baled out of their tanks, were killed while returning to their own lines. Contemporary accounts would suggest a Soviet loss of three T-26s. By 1000hrs, the attack was over.

It had been an expensive business for the Finns, and the remaining tanks of the company (those that had broken down before the battle) were later transferred to the Rautalampi sector to serve in an anti-tank role. Honkaniemi illustrated that the Finns were too inexperienced and underequipped to try to engage the Soviets in tank-on-tank action. Locally, they were outnumbered by Soviet units, who were

A Soviet heavy machine-gun support unit. By 1940, having established a base of fire with such units, Soviet infantry could advance under cover of fire support, unlike many of the attacks early in the war. (Sovfoto/Universal Images Group via Getty Images)

9   In an effort to save money, the Vickers tanks had been bought without radios, weapons, gun sights and, in some cases, driver's seats. This equipment was fitted on the Finnish side but not with a radio in every tank. This was a common problem at the beginning of World War II for all nations. In some Soviet tank units only one in three tanks had a radio, making it impossible for a section commander to communicate with his tanks once an engagement started.

experienced in handling their tanks in battle and who also travelled with their own AT guns. In the weeks that followed, the Finns would find that their opponents were becoming more proficient on the battlefield and this would put their forces under increasing pressure along all fronts.

BREAKING THE MANNERHEIM LINE, FEBRUARY 1940

Early to mid-January 1940 marked what was perhaps the lowest point in terms of the Soviet effort. While Soviet divisions were being decimated along the Raate Road, apparently beyond the help of other Soviet forces in the sector, the campaign stalled on all fronts. In the depths of winter, the Finns were perfectly happy to downscale operations, survive in the extreme weather and occasionally engage in hit-and-run attacks on the Soviet forces. The Soviet plan had been totally derailed and none of the major objectives had been achieved. The initial timetable had been wildly optimistic, with a victory planned for 21 December 1939 to coincide with Stalin's birthday. The Soviet propaganda machine was in overdrive trying to explain the lack of progress, blaming the climate and terrain while also claiming that the Mannerheim Line was much stronger than it actually was. The Soviets also claimed that the USA had sent 1,000 crack pilots to Finland to help the war effort. But in operational and tactical terms, it was obvious that a major rethink was required.

Firstly, the chief of staff of the entire Red Army – Army Commander, 1st Class Boris Shaposhnikov – was given full authority over the Finnish campaign. In late December 1939, he ordered the suspension of all frontal assaults on the line and began a phase of assessment and reorganization. On 7 January 1940, Army Commander, 1st Class Semyon K. Timoshenko was appointed to command the renamed North-Western Front. He was a competent tactician and excellent organizer, and his appointment would become synonymous with later Soviet successes. Timoshenko brought considerable energy and focus to a major programme of retraining and reorganization. He knew that the Soviets had all the elements required to

A section of the Mannerheim Line on the Karelian Isthmus, showing outlying sections of wire and also 'dragon's teeth'-type anti-tank obstacles. Looming on the hill in the background, the SJ5 or 'Millionaire Bunker' dominates the terrain. In January 1940, the Soviet command planned complex, combined operations to overcome such positions. (SA-kuva)

break the Mannerheim Line, but that they were not being used properly. There was intense training in coordinating combined-arms operations with an increase in the number of forward air and artillery observers. Life-size mock-ups of sections of the Finnish defences were constructed and these were used for large-scale exercises and rehearsals, many of which included 'live fire' phases. There were division-size signals exercises to plan for better coordination of air and artillery fires. Timoshenko also realized that the existing Soviet tactical doctrine needed to be altered to compensate for the Finnish conditions.

There was a vast re-equipping of the Soviet forces in the North-Western Front with large numbers of tanks, artillery and aircraft arriving in early 1940. These supplemented existing formations and the force was reorganized into two armies: 7th Army (14 Rifle divisions) and 13th Army (nine Rifle divisions). Supporting the 7th and 13th armies were five tank brigades, 15 air regiments and over 2,800 artillery guns. In total, there were now over 600,000 troops available for the renewed effort. Soviet propaganda would later claim a huge surge in the morale of the Soviet troops. It is difficult to ascertain the veracity of these claims, but it is true that Soviet

Generals Timoshenko and Zhukov during the autumn exercises in 1940. Having overcome major setbacks in Finland, Timoshenko would emerge as one of the main Soviet military commanders in World War II. (Sovfoto/ Universal Images Group via Getty Images)

troops displayed a high degree of focus, courage and professionalism in the offensives of 1940. As Timoshenko oversaw this phase of preparation, he was further aided by Stalin, who seems to have adopted a more realistic attitude to the difficulties of the Finnish campaign. Stalin and Timoshenko were on reasonably friendly terms, and the general was provided not only with the military assets required but also time to prepare his plans.

For the upcoming attack, Timoshenko's main effort would fall in the sector known as the 'Viipuri Gateway'. The terrain of the Karelian Isthmus was extremely problematic, with numerous water obstacles, areas of marshland and poor roads. In the vicinity of the villages of Summa and Lähde there was a 16km-wide gap that was unimpeded by marshland or heavy forest. There were also a number of roads in the sector that would aid a Soviet advance in the direction of Viipuri, which had been an early and key Soviet objective. There was, however, the small problem of the Mannerheim Line, which was strong in this area, as the Finns had spotted the potential of the Viipuri Gateway. Included in the fortifications here were the two strong bunker fortifications known as the Millionaire and Poppius bunkers. The sector also had extensive trenchworks, bunkers, minefields and wire obstacles, while the Finns had scoped out the terrain very accurately to allow for efficient MG, mortar and artillery fire. To counter Soviet tanks the Finns had some of the precious 37mm Bofors AT guns in the sector, and some sections of terrain had been deliberately flooded to further impede movement. Despite the shortages of men, ammunition and equipment faced by the Finns at this stage of the war, they had created an extremely difficult battlespace for the

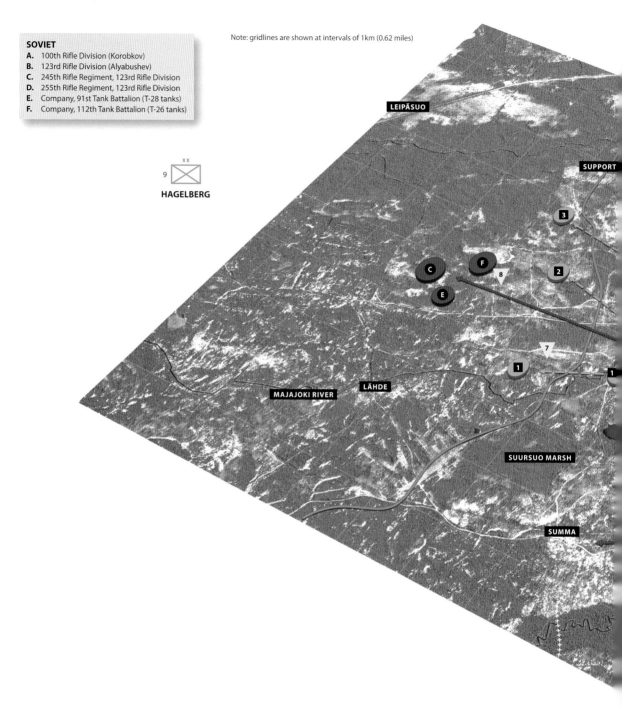

Note: gridlines are shown at intervals of 1km (0.62 miles)

SOVIET

A. 100th Rifle Division (Korobkov)
B. 123rd Rifle Division (Alyabushev)
C. 245th Rifle Regiment, 123rd Rifle Division
D. 255th Rifle Regiment, 123rd Rifle Division
E. Company, 91st Tank Battalion (T-28 tanks)
F. Company, 112th Tank Battalion (T-26 tanks)

9 XX

HAGELBERG

LEIPÄSUO

SUPPORT

LÄHDE

MAJAJOKI RIVER

SUURSUO MARSH

SUMMA

EVENTS

1. 11 February 1940: The two Soviet rifle divisions move to their initial positions. The 100th Rifle Division is tasked with taking Summa, the 123rd Rifle Division with seizing the Millionaire and Poppius bunkers of the Mannerheim Line.

2. 11 February 1940, 1100hrs: The 245th and 255th Rifle regiments launch their attacks on the Millionaire and Poppius bunkers respectively, supported by elements of the 91st and 112th Tank battalions. 255th Rifle Regiment's attack stalls.

3. The 245th Rifle Regiment, attacking over swampy ground, is unable to employ armoured support, and is pushed back with heavy losses.

4. 11 February 1940, 1200–1400hrs: Having attacked again, the 245th Rifle Regiment succeeds in clearing the Poppius Bunker.

5. The Finnish companies under Malm and Hannus fall back behind the Support Line.

6. The Millionaire Bunker is under increasing pressure from 255th Rifle Regiment. Between 0000hrs and 0500hrs on 12 February 1940 (according to Finnish sources, 13 February), the regiment manages to surround the bunker. Soviet combat engineers succeed in placing charges on it, and it is captured around 0500hrs.

7. Ericsson's company is too weak to retake the position, and retreats behind the Support Line.

8. The 245th Rifle Regiment, supported by the 91st and 112th Tank battalions, consolidates Soviet gains and breaks through the Finnish Support Line. This breach renders the Mannerheim Line untenable.

BREACHING THE MANNERHEIM LINE, 11–13 FEBRUARY 1940

Army Commander, 1st Class Semyon K. Timoshenko's offensive tasked the 100th Rifle Division with taking Summa while the 123rd Rifle Division seized the 'Millionaire' and 'Poppius' bunkers of the Mannerheim Line. The attacks caused heavy losses to the Soviets, but eventually they managed to break through. The breach was one of the reasons the Finns abandoned the Mannerheim Line.

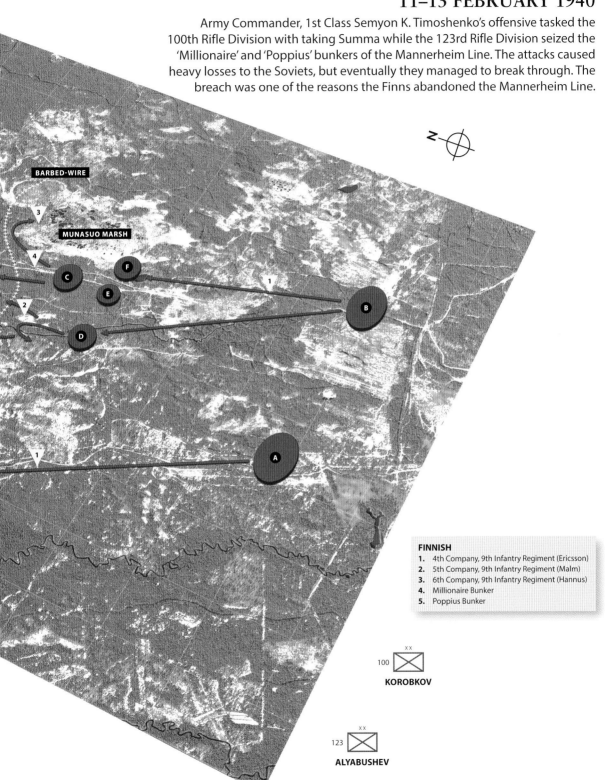

BARBED-WIRE

MUNASUO MARSH

FINNISH
1. 4th Company, 9th Infantry Regiment (Ericsson)
2. 5th Company, 9th Infantry Regiment (Malm)
3. 6th Company, 9th Infantry Regiment (Hannus)
4. Millionaire Bunker
5. Poppius Bunker

100 ⊠ X X
KOROBKOV

123 ⊠ X X
ALYABUSHEV

Finnish fortifications in the Summa sector. These are a mix of trench systems with reinforced concrete sections. Such defences posed considerable challenges for attacking troops. In other areas of the Mannerheim Line the defences were even more elaborate. (TASS via Getty Images)

Soviets. There was potential for the upcoming battle to descend into a World War I-type scenario and the Finns were confident, as they had thwarted the previous Soviet efforts in this sector.

To crack this objective, Timoshenko developed a relatively simple plan. The attack would be preceded with intense, around-the-clock artillery bombardments. The Soviets had stockpiled a vast amount of shells, and in the 24-hour bombardment that led up to the main attack on 1 February 1940, over 300,000 shells were fired. Alongside the artillery preparation, there would be constant Soviet attacks along the entire length of the line to dissipate the Finnish defenders and deny them the chance to move forces from quiet sectors. The 7th Army, the larger of the two army formations, would focus all of its strength on the 16km section of the Viipuri Gateway, attacking towards Summa but with the main effort driving into the gap between the Suursuo and Munasuo marshes in the direction of the Millionaire and Poppius bunkers. Within this front-wide offensive, the 7th Army would use its armour to punch through the Mannerheim Line; they would then keep the breach open and this would allow further echelons of Soviet forces to drive through. It was a variation of established Soviet deep-battle doctrine. Much time was spent identifying Finnish positions and strongpoints through air reconnaissance and also flash spotting by ground observers. These positions were subjected to heavy bombardment, and particular attention was given to both the Millionaire and Poppius bunkers. By 28 January, the Millionaire Bunker was already badly damaged.

Having engaged in preparatory attacks of one or two companies along the line and also intense artillery fires, the Soviets increased artillery and air attacks on 1 February. In the ten days that followed, the Finns were subjected to numerous battalion-size attacks, with several of the outlying bunker and trench complexes being lost and then retaken in costly counter-attacks. Some positions changed hands several times, but the Soviets also kept possession of hard-won territory. In this early, attritional phase, it is estimated that the Finns suffered around 3,000 casualties. The Soviet units suffered, too, but Timoshenko had enough fresh battalions to allow him to rotate them into the fight to replace worn-out units. Increasingly, the Soviets dominated the battlespace by day while the Finns were forced to carry out resupply and repair work during the night.

The main Soviet offensive began at 1100hrs on 11 February and would be followed by three days of intense fighting. The attack was spearheaded by the 245th and 255th Rifle regiments supported by two companies of tanks (one company of T-28s, one of T-26s). The 255th Rifle Regiment engaged in a fierce fight through the outlying trench system to reach the Millionaire Bunker itself, but was pushed off the position with MG fire and grenades before taking shelter in the former Finnish trenches.

Soviet tank firing on the Mannerheim Line, 1940. In the early phase of the war, Soviet armour had been hampered by poor infantry and artillery cooperation. These tactical glitches had been ironed out by the spring of 1940. (Sovfoto/Universal Images Group via Getty Images)

To the east, Soviet troops had to advance without armour support due to the Munasuo marsh. They were repulsed by Finnish troops of 9th Infantry Regiment under Lieutenant H. Hannus with heavy losses.

The fight for the Poppius Bunker was to be more successful for the Soviets. In previous armoured attacks, Soviet tanks had displayed a tendency to charge forward and act without infantry support. This fault had been rectified in the training programmes of January 1940. Units of the 245th Rifle Regiment now advanced on the Poppius Bunker and maintained close contact with their tank support. This denied the Finnish tank-destroyer teams the opportunity to engage the tanks with Molotovs and satchel charges. Now, numerous Soviet tanks advanced, firing on the Poppius. Others manoeuvred up to the bunker's firing slits and embrasures and blocked the fire of the Finnish gun teams. These tactics forced the Finns into the open, and the defenders – men of the 5th Battalion, 9th Infantry Regiment under Lieutenant Malm – engaged the attacking troops with small arms and grenades. It was a

On the left, this Finnish soldier is holding what appears to be an improvised satchel or cluster charge. This entailed explosive charges tied around a handle with a grenade incorporated as the detonator. To the right, this soldier has a Molotov cocktail tied to his belt equipment. Used in the Spanish Civil War, the Finns would develop the design and christen the device after the Soviet foreign minister. (SA-kuva)

THE ATTACK ON THE POPPIUS BUNKER, 11 FEBRUARY 1940 (PP. 76–77)

For the renewed Soviet attacks on the Mannerheim Line, locations such as the Poppius Bunker (**1**) had been recognized as being key to the integrity of the Finnish defences. Having undergone a period of extensive refit and retraining, the forces under Timoshenko's command put in an impressive performance in the Soviet offensives of February and March 1940.

The substantial Soviet air assets were put to more effective use to dominate the battlespace. Here, Polikarpov I-16s (**2**) are providing top cover and also engaging in some level of close air support. Soviet armour also performed much more competently and was properly supported by the infantry. In the attacks on the Poppius Bunker, T-28 tanks (**3**) played a key role, advancing right up to the bunker and blocking its firing ports.

The Soviet infantry put in a determined attack on the Poppius Bunker with their fire support teams (**4**) laying down suppressing fire to allow the infantry (**5**) to advance. Notably, the Soviet junior leadership played a significant role in these operations. Combat engineers accompanied the leading waves of the assault and carried out extensive demolition attacks while under heavy fire.

The fall of the Poppius Bunker was a key moment for the Soviet war effort and the Finns would gradually be pushed back through their lines of defences in the coming weeks. While hard fighting lay ahead, the Soviets had finally streamlined the use of their various combat assets to engage in effective combined-arms operations.

Soviet troops atop a captured bunker of the Mannerheim Line, near Hottinen, 1940. (TASS via Getty Images)

desperate fight and the Soviet troops took heavy losses. But at 1328hrs, the Poppius Bunker was finally overrun and the Red Banner was hoisted over the shattered position.

It was a key moment in the attack and in the war itself. Facing encirclement, the surviving defenders around the Poppius Bunker fell back, as did Lieutenant Hannus' company on the eastern flank. Soviet troops and tanks followed up and began moving towards Lähde. Furthermore, the fall of the Poppius Bunker also left the Millionaire Bunker isolated and unsupported. Assault parties of the 255th Rifle Regiment were tasked with reducing the Millionaire Bunker, but their attacks stalled due to heavy defending fire. Finally, 2nd Lieutenant Lekanov's assault party reached the bunker and used explosives to demolish the entrances and trap the remaining Finnish defenders inside (by this time, there were only eight Finns left, commanded by Lieutenant Skade).

There is some confusion relating to the timeline that followed. According to Soviet sources, they renewed the attack on the Millionaire Bunker at 0500hrs on 12 February. According to Finnish sources, this attack took place on 13 February. In any event, the outcome was now assured. There were efforts by a unit from the Finnish 9th Infantry Regiment to retake the position, but despite gaining a foothold in the trenches outside the bunker, they were eventually driven off. The Soviets then detonated a large demolition charge, effectively reducing the Millionaire Bunker to rubble.

Finnish counter-attacks from Lähde had been beaten back on 12 February, and a further counter-attack on 13 February also failed. That same day, the Soviet 245th Rifle Regiment pushed on towards Lähde, supported by armour from the 90th and 112th Tank battalions. There they broke through the Support Line and further compromised the integrity of the whole Mannerheim Line. Lacking reinforcements and crucial equipment such as anti-tank guns and with their communications network collapsing, the Finns were in a desperate position. With a gap now several kilometres deep around Lähde, the Finns knew that they would be eventually pushed back through their lines of defence. The Soviets had developed a formula that they could repeat, and they would eventually break through both the Interim and Rear lines. It was now just a matter of time.

THE AIR WAR

As was the case on the ground, the Soviet Air Forces (*Voyenno-Vozdushnye Sily* –VVS) entered the war with a huge superiority in numbers; Soviet sources indicate 3,253 aircraft in total. These included modern fighter and bomber types including the Polikarpov I-15, I-16, I-53 and the Tupolev SB (also known as the Tupolev ANT-40). While these aircraft did not perform to expectations, the sheer numbers of Soviet aircraft ensured their air dominance.

The Soviets employed their bombers in a close-support role, but due to poor communications and the lack of forward air observers it was not until February 1940 that they could be truly effective in this role. At a strategic level, the Soviets targeted railway lines, rail yards and supply depots. Due to the low level of industrialization in Finland, it was difficult for the Soviets to use their air power to target war-producing infrastructure. However, the port town of Turku, with its shipyards and also an ammunition factory, was bombed several times. Soviet planes also attacked Finnish harbours and ships at sea, and dropped mines in sea lanes.

The war began with an air raid on Helsinki, and despite propaganda claims that there were no attacks being carried out on civilian targets, there were further such raids during the war. In total, Helsinki was bombed eight times during the war with the loss of 97 people killed and over 260 injured. Viipuri became a focus of Soviet bombing operations in early 1940 and over 12,000 bombs were dropped on the city, badly damaging large areas of it. In total over 516 locations were bombed during the war, inflicting over 900 casualties. It is estimated that the VVS flew an average of 1,000 sorties per day during the war, losing over 500 planes due to weather, accident, AA fire, ground fire and Finnish fighter actions.

As a comparison, the Finnish Air Force started the war with just 114 serviceable aircraft, all of which were, at best, obsolescent if not totally obsolete. On some occasions during the war, due to mechanical and weather issues, the Finns had just 40 aircraft available. In terms of fighter aircraft/interceptors, they had 36 Fokker D.XXIs available and ten Bristol Bulldog IVa fighters. These were later supplemented by donations of Fiat G.50s from Italy, Gladiator Mk IIs from Britain, Morane-Saulnier MS406s from France and Brewster M.239s from the USA. These doner aircraft arrived in

small numbers and generally too late in the war to make a significant impact. In terms of bombers and reconnaissance aircraft, the Finns had a small number of Bristol Blenheims, but not enough to be effective as close air support. It is interesting that, in March 1940 as the Finns faced defeat, Mannerheim was focused on trying to secure 100 bombers from Britain and/or France. It is unclear what use he intended to put them to.

While a tiny force in comparison with other European air forces, the Finns had spent considerable time during the 1930s perfecting their tactics to align them with their scant resources. Following experimentation in mock aerial combats, the Finnish fighter regiment commander Lieutenant-Colonel Richard Lorenz recommended that the three-fighter formation be dropped in favour of a two-fighter formation. These pairs could be augmented by a further pair to create what was termed in German fighter tactics as a *Schwarm*. The development of an advanced air-fighting theory was facilitated by the secondment of Major Gustaf Magnusson to the German Jagdgeschwader 132 for a four-month period before the war. There, Magnusson learned to operate in the German four-fighter configuration – the 'finger-four'. These tactics were disseminated throughout the Finnish Air Force. New pilots received good, but basic, tactical instruction and this allowed them to perfect specific tactics focused on attacking bomber formations. Finnish pilots were encouraged to close up on enemy bombers before firing. Fighter planes' guns were set at 150m, but in combat Finnish pilots tended to hold their fire until just 50m from their targets. Fighter-on-fighter combat was to be avoided.

Despite the huge disparity in numbers, the Finnish Air Force gave a good account of itself with small numbers of fighters frequently attacking large bomber formations. On one occasion (6 January 1940) Lieutenant Toma Sarvanto managed to shoot down six Soviet bombers in an action that lasted just four minutes. In total, the Finnish Air Force flew 5,693 sorties during the war, claiming 207 Soviet aircraft destroyed for a loss of 53 of its own. Finnish air-defence artillery claimed a further 314 aircraft shot down. Soviet sources claimed 427 Finnish planes shot down, which is more than the Finns ever possessed, while admitting a loss of 579 of their own. Ultimately, this was an air campaign that was followed with intense interest by the international press and also by air force commanders across the globe. Against the backdrop of World War II, with increasing levels of air activity by all the

A Finnish pilot and his Fokker D.XXI fighter during the Winter War. With its fixed landing gear, these fighters were a generation behind their Soviet counterparts, yet still managed to achieve some kills. (SA-kuva)

The Winter War opened with a Soviet air raid on Helsinki on 30 November 1939. Timed to coincide with the 'rush hour' period, the Soviet attack resulted in many civilian casualties. There were seven further raids on Helsinki during the war, resulting in over 90 dead and over 260 wounded. (Fox Photos/Hulton Archive/Getty Images)

belligerent nations, the theorists of both strategic bombing and fighter defence pored over the reports from the Winter War in the hope of drawing applicable lessons.

THE WAR AT SEA

Due to the timing of this campaign, there was comparatively little naval activity due to worsening weather and the gradual development of sea ice, especially off the Finnish northern coast. This was perhaps just as well for the Finns: they had only a small navy consisting of two coastal defence vessels and a small number of patrol vessels, gunboats, minelayers and minesweepers. It was designed as a coastal defence force and in no way could have challenged the two Soviet fleets earmarked for this operation: the Northern Fleet and the Baltic Fleet.

From 30 November 1939, the Northern Fleet cooperated with the divisions of the Soviet 14th Army in their operations to seize Petsamo, Liinahamari harbour and the Rybachi Peninsula. As part of the initial operation, units of the 52nd Division were transported to Petsamo by sea and Soviet naval infantry supported the landing. While the 14th Army pushed the Finnish defenders further southwards over the succeeding weeks, the Northern Fleet remained on station and on high alert, as it was thought that Britain and France might try to land an intervention force near Murmansk.

For the Soviet Baltic Fleet, the war was a relatively uneventful one and it is interesting to speculate if a positive outcome could have been achieved sooner if the Soviets had used their naval assets more aggressively. On several occasions, harbour towns and coastal defences were shelled by vessels of the Baltic Fleet, but there was no major action or attempt at a landing.

An unusual aspect of the war was the Finnish engagement of Soviet surface units using coastal artillery. This happened on various occasions in the war, most notably near the island of Russarö (south of Hanko) on 1 December when the cruiser *Kirov* was shelled by Finnish coastal artillery. The *Kirov* was hit and damaged with a loss of 17 dead. On other occasions, coastal batteries engaged land targets to some effect.

The Finns also had five submarines and had been developing a large submarine type since the early 1930s in cooperation with a Dutch company,

Ingenieurskantoor voor Scheepsbouw (IvS). In reality, IvS was a front for a German naval project and the ruse was designed to get around the submarine ban placed on Germany after the Versailles Treaty. The prototype, the *Vesikko*, was launched in 1933 and served as the basis for the slightly larger Vitehinen class of three boats. The *Vesikko* made several sorties during the war in an effort to intercept Soviet surface units. These were unsuccessful due to its slow submerged speed.

The *Saukko* had been completed in 1930 and, with a displacement of just 99 tons and a crew of 15, was officially then the world's smallest submarine. Designed with use in Lake Ladoga in mind and featuring a special hull to protect against ice, it served during the war in the Gulf of Finland and carried out minelaying duties. It is known that on one occasion, 8 December 1939, it sortied against a Soviet destroyer group that was shelling coastal positions. It was too slow to make contact. As winter set in, ice conditions made further submarine operations impossible for all of the Finnish submarines. Despite this comparative lack of success, elements of the two Finnish designs, especially those of the *Vesikko*, were later incorporated into the German Type II U-boat design.

An anti-aircraft position on a Finnish naval vessel. Due to the timing of the campaign, naval action was limited, as ice conditions restricted the movements of both navies. This was perhaps just as well for Finland, as the Soviet Navy had potentially an overwhelming superiority both in the Baltic and Barents seas. (SU-kuva)

The Finnish submarine *Vesikko* surfaces in a photo taken in August 1941. Launched in 1933, this submarine was developed in Finland by a Dutch engineering company that was, in reality, a German-backed operation. The *Vesikko* saw limited operations during the Winter War of 1939–40. (SA-kuva)

Finnish trench lines in the Kuhmo sector in February 1940. Often located within forested areas, such positions were hard to target with artillery. The reinforcement with timber elements made these positions more resistant to Soviet fire. (SA-kuva)

ENDGAME, 15 FEBRUARY–13 MARCH 1940

It is an interesting aspect of the Winter War that, while the situation was deteriorating on the Karelian Isthmus, the Finns were still managing to resist in other sectors. Throughout February, the Soviets found the going tough in the Kollaa and Kuhmo sectors, while in other locations their troops were trapped in *motti*. Following the breakthrough of the Mannerheim Line defences near Lähde, however, the final outcome was more or less assured. By 15 February, Finnish troops were falling back on the Interim Line, and following a gradual build-up and intense fighting, Soviet forces passed over this line of defences on 28 February.

The fight now turned to Viipuri and the incomplete defences of the Rear Line. With the Finnish right anchored on Viipuri Bay, the defensive line ran through the city of Viipuri to the Vuoski River with the result that both flanks were protected to some degree. Meretskov's Soviet 7th Army was tasked with carrying out attacks on both flanks and also in the centre of the Finnish line. He ordered the 10th and 28th Rifle corps to advance to the west of Viipuri and to cross Viipuri Bay in an effort to pass the Finnish right flank. The 19th Rifle Corps was to advance to the east while the 34th and 50th Rifle corps were to advance directly on Viipuri and the Finnish centre.

Starting in early March, the Soviet forces began to gradually push back the Finns from the outlying islands and the Vilaniemi Peninsula to the west of Viipuri. The offensive was not without setbacks for the Soviets, and at one point the 168th Rifle Division was cut off and surrounded. By 9 March, the Soviets had cut the Hamina–Viipuri Road and the 34th Rifle Corps was ordered to intensify its attack on the city as the Finns lost control of several of the outlying islands. On 10 March, the 28th Rifle Corps secured a key bridgehead at Vilajoki, while Soviet cavalry concentrated on the island of Piisaari. By this time, both sides were reaching total exhaustion, and on 11 March, some Finnish units were pushed out of Viipuri. The fighting for and in the city had been intense. The Soviet assault had been accompanied by heavy artillery and air bombardment, and large portions of the city were on fire. In this final phase of the war, the Finns showed a competence in fighting in built-up areas. As Soviet troops and tanks advanced into Viipuri, they were opposed in heavy street fighting and, on occasions, Finnish troops launched Molotovs from the rooftops on the Soviets below. By this stage, the cohesion of the Finnish units was finally collapsing and the defence was led by composite units such as Group Varko. On 12 March, Lieutenant-General Heinrichs

The destruction following a *motti* action at Lemetti in February 1940. (SA-kuva)

ordered a withdrawal from the Viipuri defences. The fighting around the city had taken place against a backdrop of Finnish counter-attacks in the Kollaa sector, and in some locations the Finns were still resisting heavily. But the fall of Viipuri left the route to Helsinki open and this totally compromised further Finnish resistance.

On 12 February, as the fighting was reaching a climax around the Millionaire and Poppius bunkers, the Soviet government made an initial peace overture. Further details of the proposed peace terms were sent to Helsinki on 23 February, and on 29 February, the Finnish government decided to engage in peace talks. This was as the Interim Line of defences was being overrun. A Finnish delegation left for Moscow on 6 March, and while the Viipuri sector was collapsing, the Moscow Peace Treaty was signed on 12 March; the same day, Lieutenant-General Heinrichs ordered the withdrawal from the city. Technically, the ceasefire was to come into effect at 1100hrs (Finnish time) the following day, but Meretskov continued the attack until the city was cleared of its last defenders. On 15 March 1940, the Finnish flag was lowered at Viipuri and replaced by the Red Banner. Elsewhere, Finnish troops withdrew to the new border as stipulated under the terms of the Moscow Peace Treaty. After 105 days of almost constant and intense fighting, the Winter War was over. In the weeks that followed, there were a number of victory parades and medal ceremonies in Viipuri (its name was later changed to Vyborg). In the original Soviet operational timetable, these had been planned to happen in December 1939.

Throughout the Winter War, there was much discussion about the possibility of foreign intervention, and increasingly Mannerheim pinned his hopes on that idea as the internal situation became more and more desperate. The initial invasion was condemned by France, the USA and Great Britain and also other nations, and the USSR was censured by the League of Nations and eventually expelled on 14 December 1939. By 1939, however, the League of Nations was a toothless organization and these condemnations had

The capture of Viipuri: Soviet tanks roll into the city, March 1940. (Sovfoto/ Universal Images Group via Getty Images)

This Finnish biplane of the Winter War appears to be a Hawker Hart B4 of the Swedish volunteer air wing. (CORBIS/ Corbis via Getty Images)

zero effect. In practical terms, the French, British, Americans, Italians and Swedes did eventually send aircraft and other war materiel. The Swedes also allowed their citizens to form a unit of volunteers and over 8,700 men served in the Swedish Volunteer Corps. The Swedes also sent a flight of Gloster Gladiators, with pilots (19th Flight Regiment) and also some AA artillery. It could be argued that Sweden sent the most useful practical aid, testimony to the close links between the two countries. Volunteers also travelled from Estonia, Hungary, Italy, the USA (over 350 US nationals of Finnish ancestry), Britain, Norway and elsewhere. In all, over 12,000 volunteers fought in the war. These included the future Norwegian resistance leader Max Manus, and the British actor Christopher Lee, who spent a two-week stint in the Winter War and would later serve with the RAF during World War II. Fifty of these foreign volunteers died in the war.

But the larger military intervention that was requested never materialized. There was considerable discussion within both the French and British governments about how to aid Finland and also within the Anglo-French Supreme War Council. Édouard Daladier, the French premier, linked the Finnish situation with the question of how to deny Germany access to Swedish iron ore production. On the British side, the Chief of the Imperial General Staff General Sir Edmund Ironside was developing a plan that envisaged bombing Soviet oilfields in the Caucasus. By early 1940, the differing strategic objectives had become hopelessly confused: if an operation was carried out, was it to thwart Soviet plans or hamper the German war effort? By trying to cover various strategic options, ultimately none were adequately planned for. The final plan was that an Allied intervention force of around 135,000 troops would land in Norway and pass through Sweden to Finland. Not surprisingly, both the Norwegians and the Swedes refused permission for this force to pass through their respective territories. The plan was then modified in late January 1940 and the force was designated as being composed of 'volunteers'. If Finland made a formal request for aid in accordance with League of Nations statutes, Britain and France would then ask Norway and Sweden to allow these 'volunteers' to transit their territories. The operation would begin on 12 March with a projected arrival in theatre on 20 March. The plan also incorporated landings at Namsos, Bergen and Trondheim in order to protect Allied lines of supply. Ultimately, the situation was developing far too rapidly in Finland, and the war ended before the ponderous Allied plan could be set in motion.

There is a certain air of unreality about Allied planning for the Finland expedition. As one French journalist pointed out, the Allied armies seemed unable to move beyond the Maginot Line to take the war to Germany but were now planning a complicated expedition to Scandinavia to thwart the USSR, which they were not technically at war with. Lord Alanbrooke, the future Chief of the Imperial General Staff, described the whole scheme as a mere 'wild goose' that was using up staff planning time. It is impossible to predict how this campaign would have developed had the Allied force landed. However, the Norway campaign of April 1940 would seem to suggest that the Allies were not prepared for this type of expedition at this time.

In Finland, Mannerheim was still receiving the staff of the British and French delegations right up to the ceasefire. Surviving War Office reports outline meetings in which he was totally frank about Finnish prospects and requested aid. The inability of the Allies to aid Finland during this period was a major factor in later Finnish decisions to side with Germany.

AFTERMATH

The ceasefire that came into effect on 13 March 1940 ended the Finnish-Soviet Winter War. Under the terms of the Moscow Peace Treaty, Viipuri was relinquished by the Finns, as was over 41,500km² of territory. This accounted for about 10 per cent of the pre-war territory of Finland. The ceded areas included the Karelian Isthmus and outlying islands, the north-western shores of Lake Ladoga, the Salla and Kuusamo regions and the Kalastajasaarento Peninsula at Petsamo. The Finns also had to lease Hanko to the Soviets for a term of 50 years for use as a naval base. The Soviets also later demanded mining rights to access nickel deposits in the Petsamo region. In total, over 420,000 Finns lost their homes and were evacuated to unoccupied territory.

During the 'Interim Peace' that followed, there was considerable internal debate within Finland. The former inhabitants of Karelia felt that they had been abandoned under the terms of the treaty and formed the Finnish Karelian League to agitate for the return of their homeland. There was much internal discussion in the press on whether the Finnish Army could have held on longer and on how to retrieve the lost territory. General discontent about the treaty led to the formation of 'brothers in arms' associations among former soldiers. As a counter-measure, the Finnish left founded the

A Soviet medal ceremony in Viipuri. Despite the catastrophic losses incurred by the Soviet army during the campaign, no effort was spared in projecting the final result as a great victory. (TASS via Getty Images)

The end of the war, March 1940

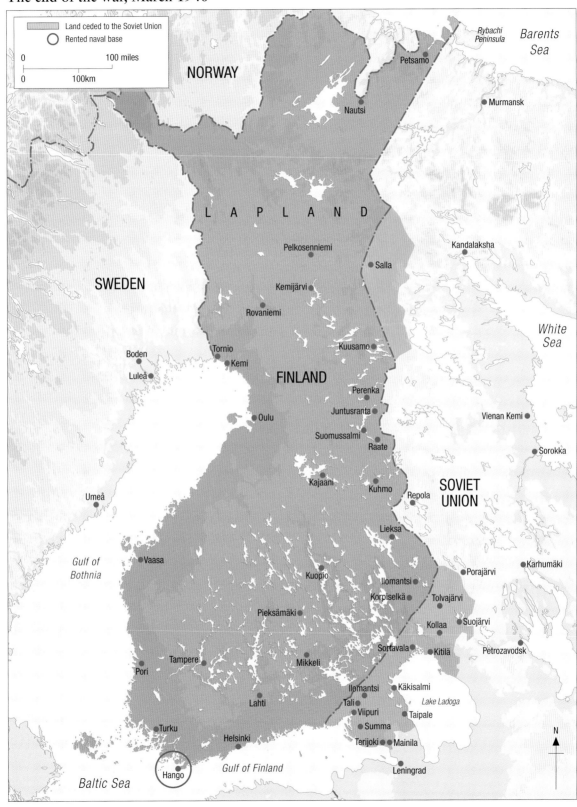

Legend:
- Land ceded to the Soviet Union
- Rented naval base

0 — 100 miles
0 — 100km

NORWAY

Rybachi Peninsula

Barents Sea

Petsamo

Nautsi

Murmansk

L A P L A N D

Pelkosenniemi

Kandalaksha

Salla

SWEDEN

Kemijärvi

Rovaniemi

Kuusamo

White Sea

Boden

Tornio

Kemi

Luleå

FINLAND

Perenka

Juntusranta

Vienan Kemi

Oulu

Suomussalmi

Raate

Sorokka

Umeå

Kajaani

Kuhmo

Repola

SOVIET UNION

Lieksa

Gulf of Bothnia

Vaasa

Porajärvi

Karhumäki

Kuopio

Ilomantsi

Korpiselkä

Tolvajärvi

Pieksämäki

Kollaa

Suojärvi

Sortavala

Kitilä

Petrozavodsk

Tampere

Mikkeli

Pori

Ilomantsi

Käkisalmi

Lake Ladoga

Tali

Lahti

Viipuri

Taipale

Turku

Summa

Helsinki

Terijoki

Mainila

Gulf of Finland

Leningrad

Baltic Sea

Hango

N

89

Finland–Soviet Union Peace and Friendship Society, which was supported by Moscow. With over 30,000 members, it engaged in activity to undermine the legitimacy of the Helsinki government and was disbanded, by court order, at the end of 1940. In many ways, considering the damage inflicted on the Red Army, the terms of the peace treaty were rather lenient. Some naval vessels were required to be handed over and the army was reduced in size, but Finland retained its independence.

For the Soviets, the aftermath of the war was quite problematic. The Finns had shown that their army was not invincible – quite the opposite. There had been problems in terms of leadership, command and control, equipment, tactics, logistics and many other aspects of their military organization. Post-war, the Soviets embarked on a major series of reforms. Traditional rank structures were reinstituted, winter equipment was improved, training programmes were reorganized and, within Stavka and the Soviet staff colleges, a conversation began as to how to develop effective operational methods to fight a modern war. None of these processes had been completed by the time of the German *Barbarossa* invasion in mid-1941.

For Finland, tough political and strategic decisions had to be faced. Before the war, there had been discussion of forming a neutral alliance of the Nordic countries – Norway, Sweden and Finland. These talks were renewed in 1940, but were opposed by both Germany and the USSR. Following the invasion of Norway in April 1940 and then the fall of France that summer, France and Britain simply did not appear to be realistic options for an alliance with Finland. Also, as the Soviets placed more demands on the Baltic States in the summer of 1940, increasingly there seemed to be one option for Finland, and that was Germany. In many ways, Germany was the net beneficiary of the Winter War. Hitler had seen the League of Nations, the Red Army and also the Allies fail at every level. It is certain that this increased Hitler's confidence that an invasion of the USSR was an achievable objective. By the end of 1940, conversations had secretly begun between Finland and Germany as to future cooperation. An alliance with Germany offered Finland the chance of regaining its lost territory while also deflecting further Soviet aggression. Such a scenario played into President Risto Ryti's vision of not only regaining the lost territory but also extending to create a 'Greater Finland', while for Field Marshal Mannerheim a German alliance made sound strategic sense. Interestingly, Finland did not join the Axis pact; its eventual alliance with Germany was specific to the Finnish-Soviet context. When Germany invaded the USSR in

Finnish civilian refugees evacuating from the Karelian Isthmus in January 1941. The war would see large-scale displacement of civilians along the border regions, and in some cases whole villages were torched by Finnish troops or their inhabitants in order to deny cover and shelter to advancing Soviet troops. (Keystone-France/Gamma-Keystone via Getty Images)

A Soviet AA battery in action on the outskirts of Leningrad in 1940. The Finnish Air Force would raid Leningrad during the Continuation War, but it is not clear that they did so during the Winter War. This could be a posed sequence for press cameramen. (Sovfoto/Universal Images Group via Getty Images)

June 1941, the Finnish Army also began operations and regained its lost territory by September, before moving beyond the pre-1939 Finnish-Soviet border. For the Finns, this was designated as the Continuation War – i.e. the continuation of their war with the Soviet Union – and it is a fascinating conflict within the wider context of World War II.

In terms of the human cost, estimates vary, but the Finns had lost between 24,000 and 26,000 dead and 43,557 wounded, of which 9,562 were permanently disabled by their wounds.

Soviet figures remain uncertain despite the best efforts of generations of Russian historians. In 1940, the official death toll was placed at 48,745. Following the fall of the USSR, archival access allowed for further research, but it is still difficult to arrive at a conclusive total. The totals offered by modern historians range from 150,000 to over 200,000 fatal casualties with over 200,000 wounded. Interestingly, in his memoirs the former Soviet premier Nikita Khrushchev put the death toll at over 1 million. Over 5,000 Soviet troops had been taken prisoner, and on their repatriation the majority were sent into the Gulag system, while over 200 were executed.

For military historians, armchair generals, wargamers and military practitioners, the Winter War continues to fascinate. As a subject, it is still taught in military academies all over the world as an example of how a small army composed of soldiers with superior fieldcraft and tactical skills, and using suitable terrain, can successfully oppose a larger, well-equipped force. The Finnish military leadership, from the strategic level down to the junior tactical leader, also offers many lessons for the modern military practitioner. It is not surprising that the Winter War was the focus of so many staff courses and wargames for NATO officers during the Cold War period.

THE BATTLEFIELDS TODAY

The battlefields of the Winter War are popular sites to visit within Finland. The war forms a significant element in the Finnish foundation narrative and has been used as an example of resilience and *sisu* for generations of schoolchildren. Within Finland, visits tend to focus on the Raate Road and Suomussalmi sectors.

Although badly damaged in the war, it is still possible to visit locations along the Mannerheim Line. Due to post-World War II changes in the border line, these are now within the territory of the Russian Federation. They do not have protected status but it is possible to visit the remains of large bunkers, such as the Poppius Bunker, and smaller bunkers and trench lines. Access to some of these locations can be difficult, so a local guide is recommended who knows the location of bunkers and is also aware of the hazards of unexploded munitions. There are several companies that specialize in tours of the Winter War sites.

There are numerous memorials across Finland, including a major installation in the main square of Helsinki. The Finnish national memorial and Winter War Museum is at Raatteen Portii, near Suomussalmi. The site also has some tanks and artillery from the war and is located in an area held by both sides at different times in the campaign. It incorporates the national memorial, which is an installation of considerable poignance. An area of the complex is set out with a rock for every soldier killed in the Battle of Suomussalmi: 900 Finnish and over 24,000 Soviet. The site also includes the 'Open Embrace' memorial structure that includes 105 bells – one for every day of the war. Raatteen Portii is a good starting point to tour the Suomussalmi and Raate Road battlefields and the museum staff can provide information regarding local guides (visit https://www.raatteenportti.fi/en/). The War Museum in Helsinki has some Winter War material on display.

Commemoration within Russia has been, perhaps unsurprisingly, more low-key. There are some specific unit memorials in St Petersburg, but in June 2000, a national Russian memorial was unveiled near Pitkyaranta (Pitkäranta) in Karelia. The site of heavy fighting in the war, the memorial incorporates a 5m-high iron cross – the 'Cross of Sorrow'. The installation was begun by Leo Lankinen (d. 1996) and completed by Eduard Akulov. It was the initiative of a joint Russian-Finnish agreement.

The new, post-treaty border near Vyborg. Given the enormous Soviet losses, the treaty that followed the war was surprisingly lenient. (Keystone-France/Gamma-Keystone via Getty Images)

SELECT BIBLIOGRAPHY

The main Finnish primary source collections for the Winter War are held in the National Archives of Finland (military records were integrated into this archive in 2008). Visit: https://arkisto.fi/index.php/frontpage?page=en/frontpage

The Military Museum of the Finnish Defence Forces also has extensive holdings. Visit: https://maanpuolustuskorkeakoulu.fi/en/military-museum

The Central Archives of the Russian Defence Ministry is a good starting place for primary material on the Red Army in the Winter War. Visit: https://eng.mil.ru/en/archival_service/central.htm

Due to international interest in the Winter War and also plans for intervention, there are further files in the military and state archives of France, Britain, Sweden, Italy, Germany, the USA and Norway.

The war was covered by many foreign correspondents, and some of the key newspapers of the period offer good accounts of the campaign. Many of these are now available online.

Finally, there have been numerous TV and online documentaries about the Winter War over the years. Among these, the 1989 film *The Winter War* (in Finnish, *Talvisota*) remains a classic. Directed by Pekka Parikka, it is based on the novel of the same name by Antti Tuuri. It focuses mainly on the experiences of a platoon of reservists fighting in the Taipale sector.

Further reading

Bull, Stephen, *World War II Winter and Mountain Warfare Tactics* (Osprey Publishing: Oxford, 2013)

Campbell, David, *Winter War 1939–40: Finnish Soldier vs Soviet Soldier* (Osprey Publishing, Oxford, 2016)

Clements, Jonathan, *Mannerheim: President, Soldier, Spy* (Haus Publishing: London, 2009)

Condon, Richard, *The Winter War: Russia Against Finland* (Macmillan: London, 1972)

Edwards, Robert, *The Winter War: Russia's Invasion of Finland, 1939–40* (Pegasus: London, 2009)

Engle, Eloise, and Paananen, Lauri, *The Winter War: The Russo-Finnish Conflict, 1939–40* (Sidwick & Jackson: London, 1973)

Gellhorn, Martha, *The Face of War* (Granta Books: London, 2016)

Irincheev, Bair, *The Mannerheim Line 1920–39: Finnish Fortifications of the Winter War* (Osprey Publishing: Oxford, 2009)

——, *War of the White Death: Finland Against the Soviet Union, 1939–40* (Stackpole Books: Mechanicsburg, Pennsylvania, 2012)

Jakobson, Max, *The Diplomacy of the Winter War: An Account of the Russo-Finnish War, 1939–1940* (Harvard University Press: Cambridge, MA, 1961)

Jowett, Philip, and Snodgrass, Brent, *Finland at War 1939–45* (Osprey Publishing: Oxford, 2014)

Keravuori, Jouni, *The Russo-Finnish War, 1939–40* (n.p., 1985)

Langdon-Davies, John, *Invasion in the Snow: A Study of Mechanized Warfare* (Houghton Mifflin Co.: Boston, 1941)

Macleod, Colonel Roderick, and Kelly, Denis, *The Ironside Diaries, 1937–40* (Constable: London, 1962)

Mydans, Carl, *More Than Meets the Eye* (Harper: New York, 1959)

Nenye, Vesa, Munter, Peter, Wirtanen, Toni, and Birks, Chris, *Finland at War: The Winter War 1939–40* (Osprey Publishing: Oxford, 2015)

Saarelainen, Taipo A.M., *The White Sniper: Simo Häyhä* (Casemate Publishers: Havertown, PA, 2016)

Sander, Gordon F., *The Hundred Day Winter War: Finland's Gallant Stand Against the Soviet Army* (University Press of Kansas: Kansas, 2013)

Sprague, Martina, *Swedish Volunteers in the Russo-Finnish Winter War, 1939–40* (McFarland & Co.: Jefferson, NC, 2010)

Stenman, Kari, and Keskinen, Kari, *Finnish Aces of World War 2* (Osprey Publishing: Oxford, 1998)

Tanner, Vaino, *The Winter War: Finland Against Russia, 1939–40* (Stanford University Press: Palo Alto, CA, 1950)

Thompson, Leroy, *The Suomi Submachine Gun* (Osprey Publishing: Oxford, 2017)

Trotter, William R., *The Winter War: The Russo-Finnish War of 1939–40* (Aurum Press: London, 2003)

Tuunainen, Pasi, *Finnish Military Effectiveness in the Winter War, 1939–40* (Palgrave Macmillan: London, 2016)

Zaloga, Steven J., *Gustaf Mannerheim* (Osprey Publishing: Oxford, 2015)

A Finnish soldier on the island of Paimionsaari, near Pitkäranta, Ladoga Karelia, in February 1940. His resting weapon is the Lahti-Saloranta M/26 light machine gun. (SA-kuva)

INDEX

Figures in **bold** refer to illustrations.